**Kiplinger Books Also Publishes:**

Kiplinger's Invest Your Way to Wealth
Kiplinger's Sure Ways to Cut Your Taxes
Kiplinger's Buying and Selling a Home
Kiplinger's Take Charge of Your Career
Kiplinger's Make Your Money Grow

# Taming the Paper Tiger

*Organizing the Paper in Your Life*

## Barbara Hemphill

**KIPLINGER BOOKS,** Washington, D.C.

KIPLINGER
BOOKS

Published by
The Kiplinger Washington Editors, Inc.
1729 H Street, N.W.
Washington, D.C. 20006

**Library of Congress Cataloging-in-Publication Data**

Hemphill, Barbara.
　　　Taming the paper tiger : organizing the paper in your life / Barbara Hemphill. — 3rd rev. ed.
　　　p.　cm.
　　　Includes index.
　　ISBN 0-938721-19-4
　　　1. Paperwork (Office practice)—Management.　2. Filing systems.
I. Title.
HF5547.15.H45　1992
651.5—dc20
92-4561
CIP

This publication is intended to provide guidance in regard to the subject matter covered. It is sold with the understanding that the author and publisher are not herein engaged in rendering legal, accounting, tax or other professional services. If such services are required, professional assistance should be sought.

Third printing. Printed in the United States of America.

*Book and cover designed by S. Laird Jenkins Corp.*

# Acknowledgments

I first shared my dream of writing this book with Florence Feldman in 1982. She has been a constant and tireless source of inspiration and support. Her professional expertise as an experienced organizing consultant, counsellor, creative collaborator and editor through all three editions of this book, as well as numerous other ongoing projects, is more valuable to me as the years go by.

Sasha Georgevitch-Taus's illustrations continue to bring a smile to my face every time I see them. The "paper tiger" on the cover by Nancy Spivak has become a seminar trademark! Patricia Hass and Susan Gies were key factors in making the original edition a reality. Brooke Ballantyne continually provides technical and emotional support on many levels, and brings much joy to my life. I am extremely grateful to Eric Kampmann who has shown faith in this book from the beginning, and who introduced me to Kiplinger Books. My editor David Harrison and his assistant Dianne Olsufka, along with Liz Reilly, Jennifer Robinson and Don Fragale have made this edition a very pleasant experience and a rewarding reality.

There were literally hundreds of clients and friends who contributed to this book, not only with specific paper-management ideas, but with ongoing interest and efforts.

Finally, the love and support of my family—my husband Alfred Taylor, my children Jenny, Thoma and Heidi, and my stepchildren Michael and Julie, continue to be a source of inspiration and motivation.

# Contents

# CONTENTS

# Introduction

I am often asked how I happened to write this book. The answer begins back in 1978, shortly after I moved to New York City after living overseas for eight years.

In searching for a way to make money and care for three children, I discovered what many others have: Successful businesses are often the result of a person identifying a need and filling it.

My discovery came while I was sitting at a playground commiserating with other parents. I'd hear comments such as, "I've just got to get organized." or "We haven't eaten on the dining room table in a month. It's covered with paper!" or, "I don't even like to go to the mailbox. I don't know what to do with all that junk." I became acutely aware that many people had difficulty "getting organized," and I realized that "getting organized" had always been one of my strengths. So I put an ad in a neighborhood newspaper, and the phone started ringing within a few days. Then, while looking for resources for my clients, I discovered that there was no book written on how to manage paper. Hence, *Taming the Paper Tiger* was born.

Perhaps my greatest fear in writing this book has been that as people read examples of how I "tame my paper tiger" they will think "But I could never be as good as she is!" Rest assured that I am *not* always able to do all of the things you'll read about. I don't think anyone can. But I think you can benefit from what's written here.

Much of my advice comes from my own experiences, both professional and personal. Before I became an organizational consultant, I held several different jobs, paid and volunteer, and entertained extensively for my husband's organization. I have been divorced—and learned to deal with issues peculiar to the single-parent family—and remarried to a man with two children of his own—thus providing me with the opportunity to experience the rigors of managing a blended family. Through all of this, I've been active in my church and in professional and community organizations. So one way or another, I've probably had to deal personally with some aspect of paper management in which you're interested!

This book is meant to be a reference that you can use time and again, as you require new or revised paper-management systems. In addition to the information available here, you will also need to add time, patience and practice. After all, very few problems are resolved by simply reading a book!

Feel free to *use* the book, which has ample room for you to make notes in the margins. I've started for you by putting lists and repeating key information there for easier access. (I've also selected short bits of advice, mottos and other things to think about as you develop your paper-management system—and scattered them through the margins of the book.) Also, underline or highlight as you read; turn down page corners that particularly interest you. Contrary to what you may have been taught, I can assure you that nothing makes a writer happier than a well-worn book!

One of the most exciting results of publishing this book has been to talk to the hundreds of people who are "taming their paper tiger." As I travel around the country, I hear about the experiences of readers experimenting with new ways to handle the paper blizzard. One of my favorite remarks is from a reader in Florida who wrote, "I have spent my entire life stepping over boxes and bags of paper. I have tamed not only the tiger, but his offspring as well!"

There is another side to the story however. Many of the letters and phone calls I receive are from people whose lives, or the lives of people they love, are nearly paralyzed by paper. They need additional help. The chapter "Paperholics" provides some suggestions.

"Organized" is not a destination, but a journey. Sometimes the road is long and rough. I have tried to write this book as though you were in the room with me and we were working together one on one. As you use this book and have questions or ideas or would like information about consulting services or seminars, please feel free to write or call me at Hemphill & Associates Inc., 2020 Pennsylvania Avenue, NW, Suite 171, Washington, D.C. 20006, (202)387-8007.

Barbara Hemphill
April 1992

P A R T

O N E

# The Paper-Management System

# The Roar of the Tiger

**W**hether you are male or female, young or old, make $20,000 a year and live in a studio apartment or make $200,000 a year and live on a ten-acre estate, you are, or will be, deluged with paper.

Do you recognize this scene? You sit down to pay some bills. You vaguely remember that the electric bill needs to be paid, but you can't remember where you put it. Your son comes in to tell you he needs his birth

certificate the next day to prove he's old enough for driving lessons. Where is it? Your friend calls to ask if you're free on the eighteenth for a get-together. That date stands out in your mind for some reason. You think maybe there's a notation on your calendar at work, but there's nothing on your home calendar.

You feel a headache coming on. There are piles of bills, junk mail, and catalogs all over your desk and night table and they seem to grow right before your eyes!

What you're experiencing is the roar of the tiger—the paper tiger.

It may feel like he is out of control, that the situation is hopeless. The truth is, you can stop this pattern—tame that tiger—with a powerful tool: a paper management system.

Paper management is a tool to help you accomplish what is important to you, whether it is finding your birth certificate when you need it, paying your bills on time, having all the papers you need when you go to your tax accountant, submitting insurance claims within the time limit, or keeping track of your frequent flyer miles.

As an organizing consultant, I have spent thousands of hours dealing with people and their paper, from parents struggling with the piles of papers their kids bring home from school to corporation executives responsible for thousands of files. One fact is absolutely clear: paper-management skills are essential to survive the information explosion in our society.

## *A Profusion of Paper*

The sheer volume of mail that confronts us daily demands increased skills in paper management. Compare the amount of mail in your mailbox today with that of five years ago. Although the computer age was billed as the "paperless age," it didn't take any of us long to realize that, although the computer does eliminate some piles of paper, it can also create even larger piles. In case you have any doubts about how the computer has affected your life, change your middle initial the next time you sign your name on a catalog order. Then keep track of the additional mail generated as a result of signing your name once. One client who tried this counted over 100 pieces in less than a year.

Just deciding what to do with catalogs is a major issue in many households. Our fascination with sleek, alluring ads for products to improve our appearance, reduce our workload, or please our family, plus our inability to decide whether we are buying or browsing, adds piles of catalogs in numerous places around the house. And don't forget all those magic money-making offers! Rarely a week goes by without the arrival of at least one "Have we got a deal for you!"

Then there is the photocopy machine. Most of us have easy access to a machine in our workplace, at the local library, or even at the neighborhood convenience store. We cut out articles, advertisements, recipes, and book reviews we think will interest a family member or a friend, and make a copy—and an extra, just in case! Then we have to decide where to keep our own copy, and how to get the other copies to the intended recipients. Unless you have a system to accomplish that task easily, the results over a period of months or years can be devastating: piles and shopping bags full of "good intentions" stuffed under beds and in closets; boxes stacked in the attic or basement; and drawers badly needed for current storage of essentials, filled instead with unidentified papers.

*What you do with a piece of paper is not nearly as important as doing it consistently.*

## Changing Family Lifestyles

**A**nother complicating factor in managing paper today is the basic change in family lifestyle. In the old days, Dad sat down at his desk at the end of each month to pay the bills. He probably never had more than five or six in a busy month!

Now, with the advent of "plastic money," the number of bills to pay each month has increased overwhelm-

*If you wait "until things calm down" before you begin to do something about the paper tiger in your life, it could be a very long wait.*

ingly. In single-parent or dual-income families, the time for paper shuffling is limited, but the amount of paper to shuffle seems unlimited: There are child care arrangements, car pool schedules, travel itineraries, shopping lists, school permission slips, house repair "to do" lists, and piles of career-related magazines and newspapers to read. Support from family members—and from household and personal services—is vital, but using it effectively requires good paper management skills.

"Blended families"—those with children from more than one marriage—can also create special paper-management challenges. If you're divorced, for example, and need to take your son to buy soccer shoes, but you only see him on Tuesday night, you need a paper management system that makes you see your reminder to "buy soccer shoes on Tuesday". It won't help to see it on Monday or Wednesday.

I grew up on a farm. I remember that as a young girl learning to cook, I quickly discovered that while it was quite simple to make every dish on the dinner menu, the hard part was getting them all on the table at the same time, with the potatoes and gravy hot, the rolls warm and the salad still molded. That was the real challenge! Paper management requires that same skill.

Most people know how to do most of the individual tasks required in personal paper-management—paying bills, writing letters, filing papers, etc. The difficult part is getting it all done at the right time. To accomplish that requires a comprehensive system.

This book will provide guidelines to help you fill in the gaps in your paper management system, or to develop a totally new one if you feel it is necessary.

Developing a personal paper-management system takes motivation, time and practice. If you have been shuffling the same piles of paper for months, or even years, it will take time to change, and it can be frightening. Accept this as "normal" reaction, not an indication that you are doing something wrong.

Digging through a pile of papers can be somewhat like waking a sleeping tiger. We discover papers that represent disappointments, obligations, uncertainty, indecision and the blinding reality that we are not able to do all the things we want to or think we ought to. Just as we have a temporary respite when the tiger sleeps, we have a temporary respite when we ignore the papers, but constantly in the back of our minds is the fear that the tiger will awake at any moment.

The results of organizing the paper in your life will be more than just uncluttered counters. As one client put it, "I was so preoccupied with finding my way through the forest that I didn't notice the trees. Organizing my paper made it easier for me to identify what is important in my life." An effective paper-management system will help you control what you do with your time and energy and create an environment that is supportive of your plans and dreams.

I do not believe that we ever set goals that are too high. Rather, we often allow too little time to reach them. Suppose you decide you want to learn to play tennis. You can buy the best book on the subject, get the best coach, use the latest equipment, wear the most fashionable clothing and go to the best court, but you won't be an expert tennis player after a few hours. Learning paper-management skills also takes time, like learning any other skill, but you can do it! And it will be worth the effort!

# Answering the Tiger's Roar

*There is no "right" or "wrong" way to organize your papers. What works best for you is the best system.*

**P**aper management means developing a system that fits your personal needs. No matter what your paper management challenges may be, there is a way for you to improve the way you handle paper—one that you create yourself for your own particular needs and life style. You may know how to handle a particular paper problem, but for various reasons you have not done so. Before long, the paper gets lost in the shuffle of more papers. You become so bogged down in all this paper that you end up not taking the appropriate action to end the vicious cycle.

Success in paper management requires five basic ingredients:
1. **Positive attitude**
2. **Sufficient time**
3. **Appropriate skills**
4. **Adequate tools**
5. **Regular maintenance**

If any component of the system is weak or missing, the system will begin to break down. Nine times out of 10, when a system breaks down, it is a sign of a changing situation, not a bad system. Perhaps the amount of paper has grown, the support system has changed, or the objectives have been revised.

## Think Positively

**A** positive attitude as it relates to paper management is an essential prerequisite. It is important for you to expect that, with the help of this book, you can and will develop a system for yourself that will suit your particular needs.

One of the most exciting aspects of being an organizing consultant is helping people create a system to fit their specific needs, and then seeing their sense of relief when they realize how much simpler their lives can be. Frequently, people procrastinate about doing anything with the paper in their lives because they are waiting to find the "right" way.

There is no "right" or "wrong" way! Many times I set up systems for other people that I personally would find very frustrating. As you read this book you will discover that there are many styles of paper management. Don't worry about how other people do it. Just look for techniques that work for you. What you do with a piece of paper is not nearly as important as doing it consistently.

To foster your positive attitude about paper management, recognize that any system you develop is a *tool* to help *you* do what *you* want or need to do. A friend of mine says, "I hate jogging; I love having jogged!" Paperwork is like that in many ways. Few people, if any, like doing it, but taking the time to set up a system means spending less time shuffling paper and more time enjoying the results—in short, taming the paper tiger.

## Tomorrow and Tomorrow and Tomorrow

**H**ow many times have you said to yourself: "I'll get organized when things calm down . . . ," "after I finish writing the report for my boss . . . ," "when the kids go back to school . . . ," "when the kids get out of school . . . " "after the guests leave . . . ," "when I come home

*Paper clutter is postponed decisions; paper management is making decisions.*

from my business trip . . . ," "when the house is remodeled," "I'll do it as soon as I have a block of time—this weekend maybe, or over the holidays." "I know . . . when I'm on vacation . . . or when I retire. . .tomorrow."

But the weekend, the holidays, the vacations come and go. As soon as one crisis is over (and sometimes before!), the next one begins. And the cycle goes on. Before you know it, you have a desk full of letters you really intended to answer and ten months of health insurance claims to submit. The desk at your office is covered with memos unfiled and business journals unread. The attic and basement are filled with magazines that never got read while they were in the den (but that contain wonderful articles and recipes). And it's April 10th, and you have no idea where your income tax forms are stashed. Many a client has called after being retired for several months, or even years, saying "I still don't have the time."

If you wait "until things calm down" before you begin to do something about the paper tiger in your life, it could be a very long wait.

## Decide to Decide

There is a very simple axiom regarding paper: Paper clutter is postponed decisions; paper management is making decisions.

Papers pile up on our counters, tables and desks because there are decisions we need to make about them. "Do I really need to keep this letter from my lawyer about my father's estate?" "Where should I keep my will?" "What do I do with all those family photographs my mother gave me for safekeeping?" "How can I find that recipe I saw in *Gourmet* magazine when I want it?" "What should I do with health insurance statements?" "Where do I put the operating instructions for the new garage door opener?"

Paper itself is not the problem. Paper is a *symptom* of a problem. Every time you ask one of the above questions without making a decision—a reply—and then taking the appropriate action, you have left some unsettled business. Postpone a few of the decisions, and a new pile is born.

## Four Questions to Ask About Every Piece of Paper

1. Do I *really* need to keep this?
2. *Where* should I keep it?
3. How *long* should I keep it?
4. How can I *find* it?

Each of these questions requires making a decision. But many people run into trouble here. Why are these decisions so difficult for us to make? There are two major reasons—lack of information and fear of failure.

## Information Please

Even though paper management is an essential skill in the twentieth century, few people have had an opportunity to learn these skills in a formal way. It simply is not taught.

The purpose of this book is to help you recognize the paper-management problems in your life, to motivate you to do something about them, and to provide you with the tools to find solutions and develop systems.

The place to begin is with the questionnaire on the following pages. I developed it as the starting point for my clients, so get a pencil and let's get going!

By completing the questionnaire, you'll identify the areas of paper management you believe are your weak spots; any score of 3 or higher indicates you could use some help in that area. Look at the last column of the questionnaire to find out the chapters that address your weak spots and turn to them.

Each chapter is complete within itself. You do not need to read the entire book to be able to put it to work

## Paper-Management Skills Survey

When I meet with a new client, the first thing I do is have the client fill out this questionnaire to determine what areas of paper management need work. Answer the questions yourself. Any question that gets a 3 or higher indicates an area where you need help. The right-hand column tells which chapter to go to.

| Strongly Agree 1 | Agree 2 | Uncertain 3 | Disagree 4 | Strongly Disagree 5 |
| --- | --- | --- | --- | --- |

| Issue | Rating | See Chapter |
| --- | --- | --- |
| I have an accessible and comfortable place in my home where I do paperwork. | 1 2 3 4 ⑤ | 3 |
| I have the "paper-management tools" (stationery, office supplies, etc.) I need. | 1 2 3 4 ⑤ | 3 |
| I have a calendar system that works for me and my family. | 1 2 3 4 ⑤ | 7 |
| I can easily find names, addresses and phone numbers when I need them. | 1 2 3 4 ⑤ | 9 |
| I have a billpaying system that works for me. | 1 2 3 4 ⑤ | 13 |
| I have a filing system that works for me, and can be used by others if necessary. | ① 2 3 4 5 | 11 |
| I can find family records (medical, educational, etc.) whenever I need them. | 1 ② 3 4 5 | 17 |
| I am comfortable with my records of charitable donations. | 1 2 3 ④ 5 | 13 |
| I am confident my tax records are adequate for the IRS. | ① 2 3 4 5 | 14 |
| I keep good records of household and automobile repairs and maintenance. | 1 2 ③ 4 5 | 11 |
| I have a large wastebasket I can reach when doing my paperwork. | 1 2 3 4 ⑤ | 3 |

**Strongly Agree 1**     **Agree 2**     **Uncertain 3**     **Disagree 4**     **Strongly Disagree 5**

| Issue | Rating | See Chapter |
|---|---|---|
| I can find warranties and directions for appliances when I need them. | 1 (2) 3 4 5 | 17 |
| I am comfortable with my records of magazine and newspaper subscriptions. | 1 2 (3) 4 5 | 22 |
| I am comfortable with the newspapers and magazines around my house. | (1) 2 3 4 5 | 15 |
| I like the way my recipes are organized. | 1 2 (3) 4 5 | 19 |
| I have enough space for books, and I can find one when I want or need it. | 1 (2) 3 4 5 | 3 |
| I organize my photographs and other family memorabilia to my satisfaction. | (1) 2 3 4 5 | 18 |
| I can easily reach the telephone when I am working. | 1 2 3 4 (5) | 3 |
| I am comfortable with the amount of time I spend retrieving information. | 1 2 3 (4) 5 | 11 |
| I can find the information I called about when my phone call is returned. | 1 2 3 (4) 5 | 10 |
| I have a "To Do"-list system that works for me. | 1 (2) 3 4 5 | 8 |
| I take some action on a piece of paper every time I pick it up. | 1 (2) 3 4 5 | 5 |
| I am comfortable with the amount of paper I throw away or recycle. | 1 2 (3) 4 5 | 6 |
| I keep up with my letter writing to my satisfaction. | (1) 2 3 4 5 | 16 |
| I can find travel information or records whenever I need or want them. | 1 (2) 3 4 5 | 21 |
| I am comfortable with the way I handle my children's records and memorabilia. | 1 2 (3) 4 5 | 20 |

*If you don't know you have it, or you can't find it, it is of no value to you!*

for you, but do read the entire chapter before you begin trying a new system. Use this as a reference book, not only when you are first setting up a system, but to refer to as you outgrow existing systems, and find you need to make revisions.

## But . . . What If?

The second major reason people have difficulty making decisions about what to do with their papers is fear. You are afraid that your decision will be proven wrong, that you will regret the decision you made, or that someone will be disappointed or hurt by your decision. You ask yourself: "What if I get audited by the IRS and I don't have what I need?" "What if I throw something away and it turns out to be very valuable?" "What if my children want or need this information someday?" "What if I file this important document and then I can't find it?"

It is not easy to answer the "what ifs" correctly. Most of us have, at one time or another, thrown out something we wind up needing later on. But here are the facts: 1) If your paper tiger is big enough, you can't find most of your paper anyway; and 2) Almost everything is replaceable. You can probably get another copy if you really need to, and, if you don't *really* need to, then it probably wasn't worth the clutter it would have caused in the first place. Remember Hemphill's Principle: "If you don't know you have it, or you can't find it, it is of NO value to you!"

## No Magic in Insight

Suppose you can take the time to set up a system, and you know what you need to do, but you just don't want to do it? What then?

There is no magic in insight! Just because you know there is a better way, doesn't mean you will do it.

You need to take action on your insight. I know that if I exercise at least twenty minutes a day, three times a week, I will feel better, look better and live longer—but that does not make me ride my bicycle or jog with my daughter.

In fact, we frequently do not act on our insights— until a crisis forces us to do so. We become concerned about our eating habits when the doctor says our life is at risk if we do not. Similarly, we decide to do something about a messy desk when we recognize that it doesn't work for us anymore. One client decided to do something about his paper tiger when the penalty on his overdue inheritance-tax bill became larger than his annual income and he was threatened with jail! What price are you willing to pay before you act?

Ultimately you will have to make the decision to tame the tiger yourself. The most I can do is point out how chaotic the alternative is and show you ways to create a system that works for you. No doubt you know that already, or you wouldn't be reading this. *Taming the Paper Tiger* will give you answers to questions and guidelines to use that will help you form your own system for managing the paper tiger in your life. The rest is up to you.

CHAPTER

THREE

# Get Centered

*If you want to tame that tiger, you have to start by putting him in a cage.*

It's Monday. You arrive home from work or from the afternoon soccer carpool feeling exhausted and rushed to get to a 7:30 p.m. meeting. You grab the mail out of the box and glance at it while you drink a quick cup of coffee.

You begin making piles on the kitchen table: one for trash because there isn't a wastebasket within reach; one for bills you need to pay; another for things you want

to read, etc. But before you can get through all the mail, the phone rings. You answer it. By the time you finish your conversation, it's time for dinner. You scoop everything up—trash and all, since there isn't time to determine which pile is which—and put it in the bay window.

On Tuesday you sit down in the family room to read the mail. The children are watching TV, and you want to spend a little time with them before dinner. The routine is the same. You get distracted. But this time the pile goes on the coffee table.

On Wednesday the mail winds up on the table beside your bed because you want to talk to your spouse before your business trip.

By the end of the week, you have six piles of mail around the house, half-opened, half-read and cluttering every room. But you can't find the bill you planned to pay yesterday or the tickets that you need for the game tonight!

The first step in solving your paper-management problem at home is to establish a location where you will routinely handle all paperwork. (Of course, if you're trying to get control of the paper in your office, you already have a location, but it may be hidden by the paper! You can start solving your problems there by organizing the desk as you would the one you need at home.) If you want to tame that tiger, you have to start by putting him in a cage.

I strongly urge you to set up a *permanent* center for your paperwork that will be available to you at *all* times. At seminars I give for managing paper at the office, one of the most frequent comments I hear from participants is, "It's even worse at home!" I ask them, "Where do you do your paperwork at home?" Typically, the response is "sometimes here . . . sometimes there."

Therein lies a major part of the problem! It fascinates me that nearly everyone has a specific location in their home devoted to the preparation of food. Many fewer people have a specific location devoted to the handling of paper. Yet most people spend as much or more time handling paper than they do preparing food!

*Nearly everyone has a specific location in their home devoted to the preparation of food. . . but many have no similar place devoted to the handling of paper.*

17

*If at all possible, establish a permanent location that can be used exclusively for managing your paper.*

Just taking your mail to a central place will eliminate scattered piles of paper, misplaced bills and checks, and forgotten notices. One class participant was amazed at how much easier her life became once she established a work area in the kitchen with a desk, a telephone and a file cabinet.

"How can that be so important?" you may ask. Have you ever tried to repot a plant in the kitchen sink using a tablespoon because you didn't feel like going to the basement to get the proper tool? Have you ruined a jacket trying to remove a spot on your suit without the proper cleaner? It's no different from the many times you opened an invitation to a party that you wouldn't think of missing, but procrastinated about RSVPing because the telephone was in the other room. Have you mailed a bill a week later than you planned to because you kept forgetting to buy stamps?

When I was a child growing up on a Nebraska farm, my father used to tell me that half the battle in getting any job done is having the right tool. The same is true in paper management.

## Choose Your Paper Place

The first thing to consider in choosing a place for handling your papers is a comfortable location. If you like sunshine or have allergies to mold, an unfinished, dark basement is not likely to be satisfactory. If you like to be in the mainstream of family activity, the family room may be an excellent location. But maybe you're easily distracted or you'd like a quiet place to go to after a hectic day at the office. Then an out-of-the way bedroom or a study will probably work better. If you have small children, you could set up your work center in an area where they can play while you work.

Paperwork under the best of circumstances is not much fun, and you will not be encouraged to do it if you dislike your work area. So do whatever you can to make it a place you like to be. Get a radio or tape player if you like music; put a cushion on your chair; or get a new lamp to put on your desk.

Many people would rather not set aside a separate space for a work area, preferring to use the kitchen or dining room table. Others have no option but to use these tables because of space constraints. However, if at all possible, establish a permanent location that can be used exclusively for managing your paper. You do not want to have to constantly interrupt the bill-paying process because the table has to be cleared of your paperwork and set for dinner.

## A Desk Is a Desk Is a Desk?

Does it matter what type of desk or desk arrangement you designate for your work center? Yes, very much so. Some desks simply do not *work* for you. The key word is "functional."

Many homes have desks that are lovely to look at and horrible to use. A rolltop desk, for example, while very beautiful, is difficult for most people to use because of the limited work space, and the numerous cubbyholes soon become catch-alls for unidentified papers. If you are going to use such a desk, be sure to label the various compartments: one for envelopes, one for postcards, one for stamps, and so on.

Some people love those beautiful secretary desks— love to look at them, that is. The biggest disadvantage to this type of desk is its small size. The best way to use a secretary is to designate it for a particular paper project, such as personal correspondence. If you are particularly fond of the desk or it has sentimental significance, this will be an advantage. You will like to go there, and you will therefore be more inclined to write personal letters. Keep all your note paper and stationery there, or at least a supply of any different styles you may use, as well as any greeting cards you have purchased. Put letters you want to answer in one spot. When the pile starts to build up, you know it's time to make an appointment with

**Action Notes**

## Equipment List

Desk
Chair (preferably on
  rollers)
File cabinet or file
  boxes
Lamp
Telephone
"To Sort" box
"To File" box
"Out" box
Wastebasket/
  recycling boxes

### Optional Equipment

Typewriter or
  computer on
  typewriter table
Answering Machine
Bulletin Board
Calculator
Fax Machine
Photocopy Machine
Postage Scale

yourself to write letters. Put your favorite picture post-cards there as well. You will be able to answer a letter, write a quick thank you note, or send a birthday card in the five minutes you have before the taxi comes or before you drive the carpool.

One of my clients had four desks and *none* of them worked. Her first assignment was to choose the one she liked most, get some boxes and empty it entirely. From that point, we started over to make not only a desk that she liked, but a desk that worked!

Obviously, many of the decisions you make regarding your work area will be based on how much room you have in your home. But even if your space is limited there are numerous possibilities.

One creative and practical solution is to buy a large butcher block top or a piece of plywood and place it across two file cabinets. This creates a nice size work area—with plenty of file space for the average home.

To hold supplies such as stamps, paper, clips, pens, etc., consider buying one file cabinet that has two small drawers and one file-depth drawer. You could also look in home- and office-organizing stores and mail-order catalogs for a small drawer to install under the table top. (Drawers designed to fit under a kitchen cabinet might do very nicely.) Try a plastic caddy designed to carry tools or cleaning supplies, or get more decorative and pick up some small acrylic, wood or brass organizers.

## *Set Up Your Center*

Wherever you choose to make your work area, be sure you have adequate lighting and a comfortable chair. One client and I spent a considerable amount of time setting up her paper-management system. She understood it and liked it, yet she never seemed to get things done—until we discovered another problem. Her arthritic neck always hurt when she sat at the desk. As soon as we purchased an adjustable chair, the neckache disappeared.

If you want to be able to move around in your work area, you will find a swivel chair on rollers a big advantage. If there is carpeting, you will need an acrylic chair mat.

A major factor in managing paper is an effective filing system. (For detailed discussion, see Chapter 11.) A file cabinet is one of the best investments you will ever make. It is ideal if your filing system is located at or close to your work center.

There is a variety of filing equipment on the market—other than the traditional metal file cabinet—ranging from inexpensive cardboard boxes to costly acrylic file cabinets on rollers. The latter type are excellent choices if you can't keep your files at your work area. You can move them to your work place as you need them and roll them back out of the way when you're done. Most types of files are found in office supply stores and mail order catalogs.

If you plan to type and you can afford the space, leave your typewriter out at all times. It often takes longer to get out the typewriter than it does to type the letter!

If you have a computer, decide whether it should be located in your work area or someplace else, so that you can still work while other members of the family use the computer.

Have a telephone within easy reach at your work area, even if it means putting a 25-foot cord on the phone in the next room or buying a cordless phone. You will be amazed at how many pieces of paper you can eliminate immediately by making a phone call when you first open your mail.

If you are right-handed, you will probably want the phone on your left so that you're free to write while talking on the phone. If you're short on desk space, consider a wall phone, but be sure to get one with the buttons and the on/off switch on the handset so you can make several calls while sitting at your desk. A speaker phone option is particularly useful if you like to do other tasks while talking on the phone or when you get put "on

*A bulletin board can be a catch-all for postponed decisions.*

*People are more likely to use a large wastebasket than a small one, so choose carefully!*

hold." You may also want to use an answering machine, although you might want to keep it in the kitchen (See Chapter 19).

Designate a special place to put those items that are ready to go to the mailbox or the post office. A napkin holder works well and can add to the personality of your work space. I use a beautifully handcrafted ceramic one that I purchased on a vacation and which evokes pleasant memories each time I look at it.

You will also need a "To Sort" tray (See Chapter 5) located on or within easy reach of your desk to collect the papers that require your action when you are ready to work.

Other pieces of equipment you may find helpful are a calculator, a postage scale and a bulletin board. Be careful about that last one! For many people, a bulletin board simply becomes a catch-all for postponed decisions. To avoid that, identify it for a specific purpose, such as upcoming invitations, greeting cards, or other mementos you've received (to be changed when they become tired-looking), messages to family members, or an envelope system for credit card receipts and bank deposit records. (See Chapter 13.)

Last, but not least, a *large* wastebasket is one of the most important tools in your work area. I cannot explain why, but I observe that people are more likely to use a large wastebasket than a small one, so choose carefully! If you generate a lot of paper that is considered recycleable, consider two baskets, a large one for the paper and a smaller one for incidental waste.

## The Basic Supplies

Once you have all the major equipment you need, concentrate on getting the necessary desk supplies. Nothing is more frustrating than to discover you've run out of staples, or to find a bill you thought was paid a week ago buried in the bottom of your purse or briefcase because you didn't have a stamp when you needed it!

Be careful not to accumulate clutter such as pens that don't write well, paper weights you don't like or use, or drawers full of forgotten or unidentified objects. If you find more things in your desk that you don't use than you do, start over! Get a box and empty the contents of your desk into them, keeping only those items you use or enjoy seeing in your work area.

If you have everything you feel you will need, the first step on the road to effective paper management is complete. Congratulations! That tiger will be purring in no time.

## Basic Supplies

Calendar
Cellophane tape and
    dispenser
Correction fluid (for pen
    and photo copy)
Dictionary
Envelopes
File folders, manila
Hole punch
Labels, plain and
    preprinted return
    address labels
Letter opener
Paper clips
Pencil sharpener
Pens, pencils, marking pens
Postcards, stationery,
    notepaper
Rotary address file or
    phone book
Rubber bands
Ruler
Scissors
Self-stick, removable notes
Stamps
Stapler, staples, staple
    remover

## Typewriter Supplies

Correction fluid (if
    typewriter is not
    self-correcting)
Ribbons and correcting
    ribbon, if needed
Typing paper

## Computer Supplies

Disks for storage
Boxes for storing disks
Labels for disks
Computer paper
Ribbon for printer

# The Keys to the System

**Today's mail is
tomorrow's pile.**

Y ou have drawers full of unidentified papers, shopping bags crammed with papers shoved under the bed, boxes overflowing with unread magazines stuffed in the closet. Perhaps you haven't eaten on the dining room table for a week because of the papers piled there. At work, your office is similarly cluttered. You want to end this vicious cycle, and you're encouraged by what you've

Having the right tool may be all you need...

read so far. (Yes, there is hope for you, too!) But you may be wondering where to begin.

## Who's Controlling Whom?

Although a clean desk is not important or necessary to everyone, the ability to find information when you need it is. Perhaps you are afraid that if you clean off your desk or kitchen counter, you will forget what it is you need to do or never be able to find the papers again. Have you ever been late to an important business meeting because the memo announcing it was not where you thought it was and you had to spend fifteen minutes looking for it? If that is the case, then the paper is controlling you instead of you controlling the paper.

The solution to this problem is a paper-management system. But how do you develop such a system?

A cluttered desk indicates a pattern of postponed decisions. The paper-management system described in the next seven chapters will assist you in deciding where your paper should go. Whether you're trying to organize your office or your home, this system will help you accomplish the following objectives:

1. **Eliminate unnecessary paper.**
2. **Avoid generating unnecessary paper.**
3. **Establish a location for essential paper.**
4. **Create a method for easy retrieval of paper.**

When you have no paper-management system or when the system you do have is not working, the unavoidable problems of paper in the 20th Century are compounded. You soon discover that you are writing notes about notes you have already written because you are afraid you won't find the first one. Your calendar is bulging with notices of special events you are thinking of going to but you fail to find the notes until the event is over. You spend hours looking for that crucial piece of paper that you know you put someplace special but

*A cluttered desk indicates a pattern of postponed decisions.*

end up calling to get a duplicate because it is nowhere to be found.

## Forget about the Backlog

When I first started as an organizing consultant and was faced with a huge backlog of client's papers, I thought that I should work with the client to eliminate that backlog first and then develop a system for them.

It didn't take long to realize that effective paper management means developing a system to stop feeling guilty over yesterday's pile and do something about today's. Instead of starting with the boxes that you never unpacked from your last move, last year's magazines that you never read, or even the unopened mail from last month, start with today's mail!

## The Magnificent Seven

In my experience, every piece of paper in your life can be managed effectively by putting the piece of paper, or the information on it, into one of seven places:

1. "To Sort" Tray
2. Wastebasket
3. Calendars
4. "To Do" List
5. Rotary Telephone File/Phone Book
6. Action Files
7. Reference Files

Perhaps you're saying to yourself, "That's far too regimented for me. I could never do that!"

The fact is you can. I've worked with dozens of clients who thought my system would never work, but they discovered they can adapt it to meet their particular style.

Keep in mind the benefits of using the system. Imagine how it will feel to be able to clean off the kitchen counter when company is coming—and know that you will be able to find the credit card bill again tomorrow. Think of how much frustration—and embarrassment—you'll avoid when you're able to spend two minutes retrieving the directions to a business meeting instead of fifteen minutes trying to reach your client to get them again.

You will discover not only that it is possible to control the paper in your life, but the rewards greatly enhance the quality of your daily life.

Remember that today's mail is tomorrow's pile. Take today's mail to your paper-management center, and begin now to develop your own paper-management system.

# To Sort It Out

*If your "To Sort" tray becomes a permanent home, you're not sorting often enough.*

**O**ne of the major stumbling blocks for many people in managing their paper is deciding where to begin. One day you look at the top of the desk and decide that the situation has gone far enough. You are tired of looking at the piles of paper and spending hours sifting through them looking for important information. So you start with one pile, but before long, you come across some papers you don't feel like acting on or can't decide what

to do with for one reason or another. So you go to another pile and start again. The same thing happens.

Before you know it, three hours have passed and the only thing that has changed is the clock, which said 9:00 when you began and now says 12:00. You feel even more discouraged!

For now, ignore all those old piles. The time will come to deal with them, and you will become more skilled at doing it as you practice.

## To Sort Short

Begin by putting today's mail, or whatever pile of papers you wish to organize, into your "To Sort" tray. Do not feel that the "To Sort" tray has to be a tray. A box, bin, basket, shelf, or just a designated spot on a desk or table will do nicely.

Many people refer to this as their "In Box," but I shy away from the term. Often people are not clear about the meaning of "In," and I find mail weeks or even years old in the bottom of their "In Box." Soon it becomes a hiding place for postponed decisions or undesirable tasks.

The "To Sort" tray is a temporary spot for papers that you have not yet identified (sorted out), i.e., the mail you grabbed out of the box, the papers given to you by other members of the family, the papers picked up at a meeting or taken out of your own briefcase. In fact, at home you may need to have a "To Sort" tray on each floor to transport papers from purses, pockets, drawers, etc. to your desk for action.

"Well," you say, "there's nothing so special about that. I already have sixteen "To Sort" piles all around the house. There's even one in the bathroom! And I've got half a dozen on my desk at work. I'm very good at "To Sort" piles!" Here's where the discipline comes in. To make the "To Sort" tray work for you, you must learn to:

1) Sort short. Be prepared to keep your papers in this temporary resting spot a short time only.

2) Use your "To Sort" spot consistently.

The trick to changing your habits and making this system work is to do the sorting frequently, before the next pile begins. Your "To Sort" tray is *the* place for papers to rest until you can get to the sorting. If it is becoming a permanent home, you are not sorting often enough.

## Handle Once?

You may have heard the expression, "Handle a piece of paper only once." For the majority of the people I know, this is impossible. I think it *is* possible and desirable, however, to handle a piece of paper only once more after it has been placed in the "To Sort" tray. Remember, the "To Sort" tray is a temporary resting place. The paper should stay there just long enough for you to determine what you need to do with it next. In some cases, it will go directly into the wastebasket (See Chapter 6) or you will want to take immediate action, so one handling will be enough. But in many cases, you will move it from "To Sort" into another part of your paper-management system. Chapters 7 through 11 describe in detail the five places your paper might belong in the system.

# Mastering the Art of Wastebasketry

**W**hen you're ready to attack the contents of your "To Sort" tray, the first objective is to eliminate any paper that is easily identifiable as unnecessary. It is not accidental that the wastebasket comes at the top end of the paper-management system; if you can learn to toss unneeded paper as soon as you encounter it, you're on your way toward effective paper management.

My experience has shown that we never use 80 per

*Your ability to achieve goals is directly related to your willingness to use the wastebasket.*

Sasha

## 5 Things You Can Do to Minimize the Paper

**1.** Get off mailing lists.

**2.** Open mail near a wastebasket.

**3.** Consolidate your credit cards.

**4.** Instruct companies not to sell or rent your address.

**5.** Don't order magazines you don't read.

cent of the paper we collect! Years of dealing with people and their paper have convinced me that the ability to achieve goals is directly related to a willingness to use the wastebasket. And there is no doubt that, in the long run, your stress level will decrease as the amount of paper in your wastebasket increases.

## Enough Is Enough

**B**ut even before we deal with effective use of the wastebasket, let's consider ways to reduce the amount of paper that gets to you in the first place. Just about every day a new glut of paper enters our lives—newspapers, magazines, mail-order catalogs, bills, requests for donations, canceled checks, memos, reminders, invitations, school papers, personal correspondence, and probably the most frustrating of all, "junk mail."

Whenever you place an order from a catalog or request information about a product or a service, you can be certain your name will be passed on to other companies. Even the telephone-directory companies sell mailing lists!

If you have difficulty throwing away "junk mail" or would prefer not to have to, you can eliminate 40 per cent of your junk mail with one letter. Write to:

Mail Preference Service
Direct Marketing Association
11 West 42nd Street
P.O. Box 3861
New York, NY 10163-3861

Ask them to remove your name from their direct mail lists. This will effectively reduce your junk mail for three to six months. Thereafter, keep sending the same letter.

Many applications and order forms contain a box you can check if you do not wish to be put on the other mailing lists. Check the box! Or include a preprinted label that reads: "Do not use, sell, rent or transfer my name on any mailing lists!'' In all likelihood, the overwhelming majority of papers you receive in the mail will *eventually* end up in the garbage anyway. The issue is whether or not they will first be allowed to collect dust in your home.

**Your stress level will decrease as the amount of paper in your wastebasket increases.**

## Six Guidelines for Answering "Do I Really Need This?"

Now back to the wastebasket. Each day brings a world of opportunities—frequent-flyer bonus offers, entertainment and educational opportunities, information about new services and stores, magazines with articles you want to save (travel, hobbies, recipes, etc.). But to take advantage of any of these opportunities, you need to be able to retrieve the appropriate information at the right moment.

Uncontrolled information is not a resource, but a burden. Piles of magazines with interesting, informative articles soon become dust collectors that take up space and create guilt. A collection of information on health and exercise equipment soon takes up as much space as an exercise bicycle, but does nothing to help you increase stamina or lose weight.

Get tough. Take each piece of paper and analyze it by asking each of the following questions. This may be difficult at first, but after a while you'll run through the questions automatically, *and* you will actually begin to enjoy throwing papers out. I play a game with myself to see how many papers I can get in the wastebasket before they even make it to the desk! Here are the questions to ask yourself:

### 1. Did I ask for this information?

Much of the information we receive is sent to us automatically because of computer mailing lists, or friends or relatives send us articles they think might interest us.

**Uncontrolled information is not a resource, but a burden.**

**2. Is this the only place the information is available?**

Is it in a book you already have? For example, information about taking care of geraniums might also be in a book you have on plant care. Would it be easy enough to get the information from the library or a colleague if you decided you really needed it? Do you have an audio or video tape with the same information? Is the information stored in your computer or on a disk?

**3. Is the information recent enough to be useful?**

A two-year-old restaurant directory is of limited value. A mailing list for a party given four years ago will be highly inaccurate.

**4. Can I identify the specific circumstances when I would want this information?**

"Just in case" is not a sufficient answer. If you cannot identify how you would use the information, it is unlikely that you would remember that you have it or be able to find it. Keep in mind Hemphill's Principle: *"If you don't know you have it, or you can't find it, it is of no value to you."*

**5. Are there any tax or legal implications?**

Would the IRS request this information in the event of an audit? Is there any possibility of a lawsuit related to this information?

If the answer to all the above questions is "No," but you are still reluctant to throw that piece of paper away, then ask this question:

**6. What is the worst possible thing that could happen if I didn't have this piece of paper?**

If you are willing to live with the consequences, toss the paper immediately!

Remember: Always open your mail next to the "circular file"—the wastebasket. It will make it easier for you to toss things out, and throwing the paper on the floor beside you would only make extra work! Always ask yourself, "Do I really need or want to keep this?"

In the first few months of my career as an organizing consultant, I was hired by a highly respected professional to organize her condominium. When I opened her door, I was shocked to see piles of paper, several feet deep, surrounded by small piles of paper that were obviously multiple attempts to "get organized." Before long, she confessed that she had finally succumbed to calling me because, when the condominium association sent someone to do a routine spraying for insects he reported that her home had been ransacked! Since that incident, I have met dozens of people who have not had guests in their homes for years because they were too embarrassed by their piles of paper. Don't let that happen to you.

## *Recycling*

I would be remiss if I did not discuss the issue of recycling in effective paper-management techniques. There are a variety of recycling opportunities, from recycling individual types of paper such as newspapers and white paper to recycling magazines by giving them to organizations or individuals that will put them to good use. One client of mine had stacks of beautiful art-related magazines in her office. She admitted that she never read them but could not bear to part with them—until we found a group shipping magazines to libraries in Poland. It was quite a sight seeing her red Jaguar stuffed with magazines with just enough room for the driver!

---

### Items You Can Recycle

Magazines and
  newspapers
Old photographs
Books
Greeting cards
Art calendars

**Places to look for recycling opportunities**

Education institutions
Hospitals and
  medical offices
Retirement homes
Libraries
Churches and
  synagogues
Flea markets
Recycling centers

# Your Calendar

**The people who are most successful in managing their time make appointments with themselves to complete tasks.**

**Y**ou can eliminate a considerable amount of paper from your desks (home and office), dresser tops, mirrors, purses and wallets simply by using your calendar effectively. The key here is to get into the habit of extrapolating the information you need from the paper, entering it on your calendar, and then throwing out the pieces of paper or, if you *really* think you'll need the information in the future, filing it away.

Calendars used in the way I'll describe in this chapter not only help eliminate paper clutter, but also the mind clutter that comes from having to remember too many details and dates at one time.

## Your "Master Calendar"

It wasn't so long ago that keeping track of our schedules was fairly simple. Husbands went off to work and kept their business schedules at the office. If an after-work business appointment needed to be made, the husband—ideally—called home first to be sure there was no conflict. Wives kept the home running smoothly, keeping track of the kids schedules and making sure social engagements weren't missed.

Life is not so simple anymore. Now husbands are much more concerned with being involved fathers, too. They want to know when the next soccer game will be, what time their child's play will begin, and when the child has no school and will have to go to the office with dad.

And of course it's not just the husband who's out in the work force. More and more American families have both partners off to work each day—and both of them must keep their own schedules while trying not to create conflicts with each other's. Scheduling becomes even more complicated for people who have divorced.

The most effective paper managers I know have a "master calendar" on which all commitments—both business and personal for all family members—are recorded. If you're fortunate enough that you can keep your business life separate from your personal life, you can keep one calendar at the office and another at home. But if you're like most people, you'll need the combined business/personal "master calendar," which you might keep at home or in the office—or perhaps it will be a portable one that you carry with you in a briefcase, your suit-jacket pocket or pocketbook.

You may ask "How important is it to carry my calendar with me?" If you do not already carry a calen-

*Many people put their calendar on the refrigerator; everyone ends up there sooner or later!*

dar with you, one way to determine whether it would be helpful for you is to keep track for several days of how many times you would have referred to your calendar if you had it with you.

In addition to your master calendar, you may need other calendars for specific functions. For example, I have a calendar on the wall of my office which shows my travel schedule. But don't get caught in the trap of having more calendars than you can manage. The key to the success of more than one calendar is to identify clearly the specific purpose of each.

## Coordinating Your Schedule

**A** major complication of calendars is coordination. Keeping associates and family members informed of changing commitments is an ongoing challenge.

If you need to coordinate calendars with someone at work, develop a consistent system appropriate for your circumstances. For example, if you make some appointments and your assistant makes others for you, agree on when and how you will communicate changes. One possibility is for your assistant to check your calendar each morning. A client of mine puts one-inch removable notes in the back of his calendar so he can use them to note new appointments he makes and stick them on his assistant's desk as he goes by.

Most families find it crucial to hang a calendar in some strategic location in their house to communicate information that affects the family, such as travel and sports schedules, family celebrations or doctors' appointments. Many people put their calendar on the refrigerator, since *everyone* ends up there sooner or later!

## Putting the Calendar to Work

**H**ere's how it works. Let's say you receive a meeting notice in the mail. Frequently you can enter the information—time, place, telephone number—directly into your calendar and throw the notice away. If there is more essential information on the notice than what will fit in your calendar, such as an agenda, directions, etc., you can note the name of the meeting in your calendar and put the notice itself into "Hold" (See Chapter 10). Put an **"H"** beside the notation in your calendar, so you will know that further information can be found in your "Hold" file. (For some other handy abbreviations I use on my calendar, see the list in the margin.)

Suppose you read in the newspaper about a concert you would like to attend, *if* you get home from work in time and *if* there are no other family obligations. Put the date of the concert on your calendar—in pencil—both on the day by which you must buy tickets and on the day of the event. If you simply leave the notice on your desk so that you won't forget, you are likely to handle that piece of paper dozens of times and still not attend the concert.

If you've written a letter or memo to someone and you need to get a reply in two weeks, make a note to yourself in your calendar, "Heard from John?"

You can see that you can use your calendar not only as an appointment calendar but as a tool for effective follow-up. If there are specific materials you want to remember to check when you follow up, make a note of that directly in your calendar.

## Make an Appointment with Yourself

In my experience, the people who are most successful in managing their time and accomplishing their goals are those who make appointments with themselves to complete specific tasks, and to remind themselves to check on specific issues. For example, you are at a meeting and you agree to complete a certain task. Make a quick calculation about when you need to begin work on that task and write a note to yourself in your calendar, if you carry it with you. If you don't, put an asterisk beside

### Symbols for Your Calendar

The following are some abbreviations I use on my calendar to help remind me of what I'm to do. As you think of others that you could use, add them to the list!

**C** Call

**CW** Calls Waiting (they will call me)

**D** See "Discuss" Action File

**P** See "Project" Action File

**H** See "Hold" Action File

**LM** Left Message

**NA** No answer

your note to remind you to enter the information in your calendar when you return home or to the office. In this way you avoid creating additional pieces of paper and you will be reminded at exactly the right time.

If there is a specific task you need to do for yourself (for example, clean out your file drawer or spend some time on your "To Read" pile—See Chapter 15), make an appointment with yourself, just as you would with someone else.

Some people are hesitant to use this approach because they are afraid of becoming too compulsive. They shudder to think of themselves talking to a friend and having to say, "I need to go now. I have to catch up on my reading!" I am not suggesting such inflexibility!

Using your calendar as a time-management tool helps you to be *realistic* about your time. If you have blocked out an hour to write the minutes from your last committee meeting and you decide you would rather do something else or you have to take your child to the doctor, you can realistically decide on your options for that given day. You can write the minutes while you are waiting at the doctor's office or block out time later in the week. But do make sure you keep your commitment to yourself in one way or another!

## Choose Your Calendar Wisely

In actually choosing your calendar, there are several factors to consider. If you use your calendar as I've described, you will need to choose one with plenty of writing space. Of course, this will mean a larger calendar, and, if you do not regularly carry a purse or a briefcase, you may feel this is not practical and you will have to make adjustments. One alternative to give you additional writing space is to use the removable notes, which can be affixed to your calendar and removed when you have completed the tasks.

A second factor to consider in choosing your calendar is the format. Do you need to see the year at a glance, the month, each day, or a combination? I like a combination.

I could not find a calendar to completely suit my needs, so I combined one calendar with a part from another one. The basic calendar is a wirebound page-a-day one. In the back I added a section from another calendar that had one page for each month. I put the two together with a hole punch, reinforcements and some maneuvering. For added versatility, I bought peel-off pockets from an office-supply store and put them in the front and back to hold business cards, receipts, etc.

The page-a-day section is my master calendar. I divide each page vertically and use the left column for appointments—including with myself!—and the right column for my daily "to dos," which I can squeeze in between appointments (See Chapter 8). At the bottom of the right side I note deductible expenses. This format is particularly pleasing when Uncle Sam calls!

The month-at-a-glance section gives me room for long-range planning. It provides me with just enough space to write key words such as a client's name, the city where I'll be, my son's birthday, etc.

For a look at how my calendar works, turn to pages 42 and 43.

### Electronic Calendar Keeping

The increase in the availability and capability of electronic calendars is mindboggling. If you are totally comfortable with electronics, you may find a portable electronic calendar that you can carry in your pocket or briefcase a perfect solution.

If you have continuous access to a computer, you may decide to adopt one of the many software programs for scheduling. The new lightweight "notebook" computers are a boon to the traveler. Computer calendars are particularly useful when more than one person makes appointments for the same person.

---

**Posted: $50 Reward**

The following is inside the front of my calendar: "$50 Reward for Return. If found, please return to (my name, address and number)." Once you've used your calendar as I've described, you too will offer a reward for its safe return!

## A Look at My Calendar

Here's a sample of my composite calendar. I use the month-on-a-page section for an overview of what lies ahead (below). Abbreviations and short descriptions to let me know where I'll be (Omaha on the 18th, for example), whom I'm seeing (Douglas on the 6th), or what important events are coming up (Chris's party on the 8th). More detailed information about the appointments goes onto the day-on-a-page section, along with To Dos and expense notations (right).

| 1992 | | | FEBRUARY | | | 1992 |
|---|---|---|---|---|---|---|
| SUN. | MON. | TUES. | WED. | THURS. | FRI. | SAT. |
| **AM** | | | | | | |
| **NOON** | | | | | | |
| **EVE.** | | | | | | 1 |
| **AM** | CHOIR | KIPLINGER | B-SUE. AFE | ——HEIDI HOME—— | | |
| **NOON** | CHURCH BOARD | ANN LUNCH-BROOKE | NAPO | PICK UP HEIDI | DOUGLAS | | CHRIS'S PARTY |
| **EVE.** | K.C. 2 | HAIRCUT 3 | 4 | 5 | ASTD 6 | 7 | 8 |
| **AM** | ———— | HEIDI TO SCHOOL | | | BET'S B-DAY | USTUN | FARM |
| **NOON** | 7 YOUTH GRP | PTA | PR MTG | DAVIES | CIES | | |
| | | | | LINCOLN'S BIRTHDAY (USA) | | | |
| **EVE.** | 9 | CLUB 10 | NCSA 11 | LIBRARY 12 | 13 | TO FARM 14 | 15 |
| **AM** | —FARM— MOM/DAD ANN | OMAHA | LINCOLN | LINCOLN | ST. LOUIS | |
| **NOON** | | PRESIDENTS' DAY (USA) | | | | | WASHINGTON'S BIRTHDAY (USA) |
| **EVE.** | 16 | 17 | 18 | 19 | 20 | 21 | 22 |
| **AM** | | WP SEMINAR | BREAKFAST M.B. | | | GRAN'S B-DAY | |
| **NOON** | | | | JACKSONVILLE | | TO VA TECH | VA TECH w/JENNY |
| **EVE.** | POTLUCK 23 | D-JOHN CLUB 24 | TO JACKSONVILLE 25 | 26 | MSPBA 27 | 28 | 29 |

42

March          1992
S  M  T  W  T  F  S
1  2  3  4  5  6  7
8  9  10 11 12 13 14
15 16 17 18 19 20 21
22 23 24 25 26 27 28
29 30 31

**SCHEDULE**

# February 5
036/330

TO DO'S          WEDNESDAY

**7** *BREAKFAST – S.C./HILTON*

**8**

Reminder to take
tape to client

**9** *AMERICAN FIRE EQUIPMENT*

*TAKE PETERS TAPE !*

**10**      *OIL CHANGE*

**11**

Reminder to get oil
changed while
at client

**12**

**1**

**2**

**3** *PICK UP HEIDI/CHRIS*
*TAKE BROCHURE (H)*

**4** *DROP OFF CHRIS AT*
*MELANIE'S 2909 OAK*
*569-32.11*

**5**

EVENING *PICK UP VIDEO/*
*CLEANING*

*INTERVIEW*
*10:00 RADIO – KXLY (H)*
*509-328-7173*
*KAREN KEKOF*

**TO DO'S:**

*WP SEMINAR REG (H)*
*LM*
*CALL PEGGY 202-741-0079*
*HEARD FROM JAN (CW)*
*RE BOARD MTG ?*
*CALL JIM 202-531-7000*
*×212*
*RE FRI MTG (D)*
*PAY MORTGAGE*
*WRITE MINUTES – NAPO*
*CALL KAREN (C)*

**EXPENSES**

*BREAKFAST-S.C. 14.50*
*PARKING 8.00*

**H** = **Hold**
**LM** = **Left message**
**CW** = **Calls waiting**
**D** = **Discuss**
**C** = **Call**

Many of my clients find that a hard-copy calendar works just fine. One attorney I know carries a pocket calendar in which he notes all appointments that will occur outside his office, such as meal or evening and out-of-town appointments. He tracks all other appointments in his computer calendar.

The bottom line is that what you decide to do is not nearly as important as doing it consistently!

# Your "To Do" Lists

**M**ost of us have had an experience such as, while sitting in a meeting or trying to go to sleep, suddenly remembering, "Oh, I never called my insurance company to take John off the automobile policy!" Or, while driving home from the hardware store, we realize we forgot to get that extra house key the cleaning service has needed for the past month.

Such experiences are the basis for the proverbial

*One of the major joys of a "To Do" list is crossing items off when they are completed!*

Please Note: Notes Can Be Hazardous to Your Health.

**Action Notes**

piles of notes scratched on the back of empty envelopes, on the corner of the newspaper or on any scrap of paper that happens to be lying around. Many of the pieces of paper in the piles around the house and scattered over our desks at work are there to serve as reminders of things we want to do at some point in the future—tomorrow, next week, or maybe not until we retire!

## To Do or Not To Do

The purpose of the "To Do" list is to provide a *consistent* place to compile notes to yourself, and in so doing to eliminate many pieces of paper from your life. Dorothy Sarnoff, Chairman of Speech Dynamics, Inc., calls such a list "A depository for your thoughts."

The "To Do" list can take many forms. There are probably as many kinds of "To Do" lists as there are list makers. Some people decry the whole idea, feeling that if they write something down they might absolve themselves from doing it! In fact, making a list of the things you need to do is the first step to developing a goal-setting technique that is essential for effective life management.

Actually, the "To Do" list offers considerable creative scope. I use two types of "To Do" lists: the daily list that I note on the right side of my calendar (See Chapter 7) and the master "To Do" list that I keep in a separate loose-leaf notebook.

Keep in mind that some "To Do's" are tasks that need to be done at a specific time while others are things you want to do but have not yet determined when you can do them. For example, "Mail a birthday card to Aunt Sally" would go on your daily "To Do" list in your calendar, while a note to buy birthday cards could go on your master "To Do" list.

One of the major joys of a "To Do" list is crossing items off when they are completed. I put a check by the items I have completed on the daily "To Do" List. I always check the list from the two previous days. If I didn't get it done in three days, I stop and analyze why, and what I can do about it. One client admitted that periodically he makes lists of things he's already done just so he can cross them off!

## How To Do It

People have different criteria for what they include in their list and how they include it. Some just use key words like "Call Jerry," but what if you look at the list and you can't remember why? Others add notes about the topic to be discussed and the phone number so they don't have to look it up when it's time to call. There is also the ongoing debate on whether to separate at-home to-do's from work to-do's. Some people keep a running list, and when it gets messy or full they start over.

The more information you want to put in your "To Do" list, the more cluttered your list will become, and the less helpful it will be. One solution for this is to devise coded symbols to record progress on a task. You can use many of the same ones you use on your calendar (See page 39).

There are other options. A friend of mine uses a bound notebook of lined paper that she divides into categories (about one-third page for each). On each line she writes the "To Do's" within that category. When the task is done she crosses it off the list in another color. Then she has a permanent record of her activities, which is very interesting and can be very useful over the years. When she runs out of space in a particular category, she writes "see page so-and-so" and continues the category. There are also numerous computer software programs for managing "to do" lists along with your calendar.

## "Like with Like"

One basic principle when organizing anything is to "put like items together." Some people apply this principle to organizing lists. Put items on a "To Do" list together based on the kind of activity required. For example, group together all phone calls, all letters to write and all errands to run. When you're running errands, you won't be distracted by a list of phone calls you need to make. Or if you are trying to make a series of phone calls, you won't be bothered by a note to buy blank tapes.

Some people just keep a running list. I keep some "to do" categories in the calendar I carry with me, such as "Errands" and "Numbers," while other categories stay in the loose-leaf book at home and another book at the office. You can use temporary labels, notations in your calendar or index cards in your pocket to remind yourself to enter a "to do" on a list that is not accessible at the time.

## To Carry or Not to Carry?

A major decision regarding the "To Do" list is whether to carry it with you. The proponents of the "To Do" list on a yellow legal pad obviously find this difficult. Some people use a small spiral notebook or even index cards they can stick in their pocket. Temporary removable notes make a handy "To Do" list when you need to put a reminder in a "can't miss it" place—such as in the car, on the outside of your briefcase or purse or on the bathroom mirror.

But to really get a firm hold on the paper in your life, I strongly recommend that you carry some form of "To Do" list with you. It should be large enough to accommodate many different types of information and small enough to be practical. I created my own "To Do" book with a small (3 1/2″ by 6 1/2″) looseleaf notebook that has a pocket inside the front and back covers. I prefer the loose-leaf format because I can add and delete pages easily. I divided the notebook into sections, using the categories described on pages 49–52.

My portable "To Do" list is a major time saver. For example, if I'm stuck in a traffic jam or waiting in a doctor's office, I can use the time to plan projects, make my "To Do" list for the next day, or write a quick thank-you note. (I always carry one or two pieces of note stationery in the back pocket.) If I'm near a shopping center and I have an extra ten minutes before I need to get to an appointment, I can check the "Errands" section in my list and find one or two things I can accomplish in that time.

## What to Make a To Do About

Your "To Do" list can be divided into numerous categories, depending on your specific needs. The following are some possibilities. As you read about ones you could use, or think of others not described here, use the space in the margin to write them down.

### Birthdays

This is a good place to list those special birthdays of family members and friends. You can create a special section, or include it in "Numbers." From this list it will be easy to translate onto your calendar the days you need to mail the cards or to purchase the cards you need when you are running errands.

### Books and Tapes

This section will eliminate those torn, yellowed newspaper articles about books you have been meaning to purchase. Use this page to list books you want to borrow from the library. (If the book is checked out when you go to check it out, note the Library of Congress number when you look it up the first time, so you don't have to look it up again.) Use another page to list books or tapes you have loaned to friends.

### Discuss

This section provides a place to accumulate information you wish to discuss with a particular person. Use one page, or section of one page, for each person in your

---

### Your "To Dos"

Several "To Do" categories are described on pages 49–52. As you read them, check here the ones you think you can use. You'll also think of others that will be helpful; jot them down here, too.

- ☐ Birthdays
- ☐ Books
- ☐ Discuss
- ☐ Errands
- ☐ Gifts
- ☐ Goals
- ☐ Letters
- ☐ Numbers
- ☐ Phone calls
- ☐ Projects
- ☐ Restaurants
- ☐ Thoughts
- ☐ Travel

———————
———————
———————
———————

*There are as many kinds of "To Do" lists as there are list makers.*

life with whom you relate frequently: boss, assistant, child, spouse, committee chair, etc. Use another page to list the questions you want to ask your doctor at your next appointment, another to list the items that you need to discuss with your mechanic the next time you take your car to the garage, or another to list concerns you want to raise at the next parent-teacher conference at school.

### Errands

Have you ever gone past the appliance-repair shop wishing you had the number of the vacuum filter so you could pick it up on the way home instead of making an extra trip? The "To Do" Book has a pocket to put such receipts, dry cleaning receipts, etc. so you'll be sure to have them when you need them. This section will save you many miles of errand running.

Group errands together according to geographical area or type of store. Most people keep their grocery list in the kitchen, but if you happen to be at work when you think of something that needs to go on the list this is a great place to put it. Then when you are ready to go grocery shopping, you can combine both lists.

### Gifts

Remember the gift you found hidden under the bed after your daughter's birthday was over? Here's a place to list the gifts you have on hand—and where they are located if you are afraid you will forget! You can use another page to make a note when you overhear your father saying he really would like to have a good pair of binoculars. You might even make a list of gift ideas for yourself, in case your kids ever ask! (I post mine prominently on the refrigerator just before Christmas and my birthday!)

### Goals

Research shows that less than 3% of the U.S. population put their goals in writing. It also shows that having written goals is high on the priority list of high achievers.

Whether you are making New Year's resolutions or designing a business plan, this section provides a convenient place to keep track of your goals and your progress. Then it will be easy to check periodically to see if your life activities reflect what you said you wanted to do!

**Letters**

This section also could be divided into personal and business.

**Numbers**

Frequently the papers in our piles contain numbers we need to remember: access codes to the cash machine, the long-distance service, or the security system, social security numbers for other family members, school bus numbers, clothing sizes or table dimensions.

**Phone Calls**

Here you can list the names of people you wish to call, with the phone number beside them to speed up the process. You may find it helpful to use one page in this section for personal calls and another for business. If you need to make a phone call at a *specific* time, use your calendar, not your "To Do" list (or use both—as a security measure).

**Projects**

Planning to redecorate your living room or give a Super Bowl party? Here is a place to collect all the ideas you have. (One client puts a small sample of her wallpaper, paint, fabric swatches etc. in her "To Do" book.) Then as you begin the project, you can enter the various steps into your calendar as they need to be completed.

**Restaurants**

Here you can record names of restaurants you would like to try, with addresses and phone numbers and business hours. You may even wish to add the name of the maitre'd. Group the restaurants together by geographical area. Then if you are meeting a friend or client

**Caution!**

Clean out your "To Do" book from time to time. If lists become overwhelming, ask yourself these questions:

**1.** Is there someone who could help me get this done?

**2.** Is there a way to simplify this task?

**3.** Would it matter if I put it off for _____ days/weeks/months?

**4.** What's the worst possible thing that would happen if I didn't do this?

downtown, you can easily check your list to see which restaurant would be most suitable and convenient.

This system will also eliminate all the pieces of paper with restaurant reviews you have been saving. It's also fun when a guest comes to town and says, "Let's go out tonight." It will take you no time to choose your restaurant.

**Thoughts**

How many times have you read a quote that intrigued you or had a brainstorm about how to solve a particular problem and said to yourself, "I'll have to give that some thought?" Here you can write those ideas down, and when you find yourself caught in rush hour traffic, or waiting in the banker's office with nothing to do, you can choose "Thought" and think it!

**Travel**

This is a terrific place to put a standard packing list for travel. Then each time you plan a trip to a new city, create a special page. Make notes about particular things you want to take with you, people you want to see or places you want to go, or information about car rentals, hotel reservations, etc. Finally, make a "Before Trip Checklist" to remind you about those last-minute "To Dos," such as checking the thermostat, turning off the coffee pot, making arrangements to feed the cat, and stopping the newspaper. Some frequent travelers make an "After Trip Checklist" to remind themselves of something they want to do differently on the next trip.

Remember I said that one of the objectives of this paper-management system is to eliminate unnecessary pieces of paper. Try just these first four aspects of the system—the "To Sort" tray, the wastebasket, the calendar, and the "To Do" list—and see how many you can toss already.

# Your Names and Numbers

If you suddenly decide to take a trip to San Francisco, it is unlikely that you will even remember that the telephone number of your favorite cousin, who lives there, is in one of the letters buried on the desk. Even if you do remember, what are the chances you will have the time to look for it? Remember Hemphill's Principle: "If you don't know you have it, or you can't find it, it is of no value to you!" Many of the pieces of paper floating

*Ask yourself, "If I wanted to contact this person, what word would I think of?"*

## Tips for Saving Time on the Phone

**If you're calling . . .**

**1.** Group calls when possible.

**2.** If you call some people frequently and they're hard to reach, ask when the best time is to call.

**3.** Identify yourself and why you're calling. For example, "Hi, Jerry. This is Pat Roberts. I'm calling to find out what time our homeowner's meeting is on Friday."

**4.** If your call is complicated, make an agenda and check items off as you discuss them.

**5.** If you think you won't cover all the issues, prioritize them and start with the most important.

**6.** At the end of the call, decide when you will call again or what other way you could get information you need.

around our homes are there because they have an important telephone number written or printed on them—or because we are afraid the number might *become* important to us.

## The White and the Yellow

In our personal lives telephone numbers can be divided into two basic categories: relatives and close friends with whom we always want to stay in contact regardless of where we live; and neighbors, services, stores, schools, organizations or government agencies with whom we will no longer have contact if we move.

In other words, each of us needs a personal "white pages" and a personal "yellow pages." For many people who move frequently, it is essential to separate those two categories so when they do move it is easy to tear out the "Minneapolis" yellow pages and start "Denver."

The first step in designing a good system for addresses and telephone numbers is to determine whether you wish to separate your "white pages" and your "yellow pages" into separate systems or use one system. Your choice will be influenced to some extent by the volume of information you want to keep. If you have an active community life, a family, a career, or travel frequently, you may need more than one.

## Choose Your Listing System

The next step is to decide on the system of listing you will use. Options range from something as simple as a looseleaf notebook or preprinted telephone and address book to a box of alphabetized index cards—or its far more efficient cousin, a rotary file such as those made by Rolodex—and on to a program for your personal computer.

In making your decision, keep in mind how portable your system needs to be or whether you plan duplicate systems for office, home (more than one floor), vacation home or travel. Whatever system you choose, the determining factor in the success of your system is ensuring that you will be able to retrieve the information when you need it.

You'll probably need several phone systems. At home, you should have a complete listing of white and yellow pages at your work area. If your home has more than one floor or if you have more than one home, you will need additional systems to accommodate those needs.

In addition, you should have a small telephone book or use the back part of your pocket calendar to record the most often used numbers so you have access to the numbers when you're away from home or at the office. If you use a separate small phone book instead of a section of your calendar, you won't have to worry about rewriting the phone information at the end of each year.

### But How Can I Find It?

Do not assume that all information should be recorded in the same way. You might list a number under the name of the individual, under the name of the company or organization, by the type of service they perform, and in rare instances, perhaps, even under the name of the person who introduced you.

Sometimes you may wish to record numbers under more than one category. For example, you might have one card for Household Repairs on which you list several services. However, you might have a separate card for "Pipewrench, Peter—Plumber," or "Plumber—Peter Pipewrench." In general, though, the simpler the system is the more inclined you will be to use it. Ask yourself the question, "What word would I think of if I wanted to contact this person?" Use that answer as your key word for entering the information in your system.

### The Rotary Phone-File

If you have never tried using a rotary phone-file, I strongly encourage you to do so! If you already have one that you've inherited from someone else or yours isn't working well, start over. Don't make "organizing your

**7.** If you get an answering machine, leave as complete a message as you can.

**When you get a call . . .**

**1.** Use an answering machine so you can decide when you take calls.

**2.** Use assertive language such as, "What can I do for you?"

**3.** Be honest! If you don't have time to talk, say so. "I'm sorry, but I'm on my way out to a meeting. When can I call you back?"

**The determining factor in the success of your system is ensuring that you will be able to retrieve the information when you need it.**

phone numbers" a project for when you have time. Instead, start with a new file and add the numbers from the old one as you use them.

In purchasing a rotary phone-file, I recommend one with 3 × 5 cards. They are large enough to staple or tape business cards directly onto (that way you don't have to copy the information) and provide enough room to give you plenty of writing space. A smaller size rotary file might be just what you need beside the phone in your bedroom.

A standard format will make your rotary system easier to use. Put the key word—an individual's name (last name first), or the name of the organization, business or service—in the upper left-hand corner and the phone number in the upper right, as this is the information you will need most often. Then list the address under the key word. If the person has other phone numbers—

## Sample Rotary-File Cards

| HEMPHILL, Barbara | (202)387-8007 |
| --- | --- |
| Barbara Hemphill Associates | |
| 1718 Connecticut Avenue | |
| Suite 410 | |
| Washington, D.C. 20009 | |

(In this space you could note date/subject of telephone calls, directions to get to the office, etc.)

HOUSE REPAIRS

| Plumber—Peter Pipewrench | 222-4387 |
| --- | --- |
| Electrician—Henry Wire | 425-3098 |
| Painter—Betty Brush | 620-4487 |

SOCIAL SECURITY NUMBERS

| Barbara | 508-60-3827 |
| --- | --- |
| Alfred | 312-59-8887 |
| Jenny | 508-69-1111 |
| Thoma | 508-29-8034 |

COMBINATION LOCKS

| 16-3-5 | (GYM) |
| --- | --- |
| 15-1-7 | (BICYCLE) |

the home number of a business acquaintance or a company's fax number, for example—record these numbers as well. Be sure to note which number is which.

In addition to name, address and telephone number, the rotary phone-file card can be used for recording other useful information: key people at a business, a simple record of correspondence or telephone exchanges, birthdays, anniversaries, dates of special events.

The file is also an excellent place for tracking your holiday card list. Make a small chart in the lower right hand corner with three columns—one for the year, one for the "sent," and one for "received," where you can place check marks. Some people create a separate holiday list, but incorporating it into an existing system frequently means less work and fewer systems to keep updated.

There is no law that says that a rotary phone-file card can be used only for addresses and phone numbers. The file is a perfect place to record bits of information you'd like to have at your fingertips, such as the social security numbers for your family or the combination to your child's bike lock. If you're not worried about security, you could also list all your credit card numbers with the number to call in case they are lost or stolen. Think of the file as a "mini-file" for odd bits of information.

Rotary phone-file cards come in a variety of colors that you can use to indicate different categories.

## Today's Mail Is Still Tomorrow's Pile

If you have a system that doesn't work—or no system at all—begin one immediately. If you put it aside as a big project, for "when things calm down," you are unlikely to accomplish the task. Instead, start the new system with the next phone number you use. In the beginning, use two systems at once. As you pull information out of the old system, incorporate it into the new. Eventually you will combine the two systems into one, or the old one will become so old you will feel comfortable throwing it away.

### Emergency!

There's a serious side to organizing your numbers. If your child becomes ill from drinking a poisonous substance, you won't have time to sort through a pile of papers for the poison-control center's emergency number. Post such numbers by at least one phone on each floor. Include police, fire, poison-control center, work numbers for family members and any neighbor or friend you might call in an emergency.

CHAPTER

T E N

# Your Action Files

**There's no point in filing something if you can't find it when you need it.**

After you have eliminated as many pieces of paper as possible by using your wastebasket, calendar, "To Do" list, and telephone listing, the remaining papers will fall into one of two categories:

**Action files**

Action files are for those papers that need your attention immediately or at some point in the near future (as opposed to the "some day" projects).

Sasha

**Reference files**

Reference files are for those pieces of paper you know you will, or think you might, need at some point in the future. These files are discussed in detail in the next chapter.

The system is particularly effective if you keep two points in mind:

**A Reference File can become an Action File or vice versa.**

For example, a reference file called "Entertaining" can become an action file if you are planning a party. When the party is over, look through the contents of the file, discard material you won't need again, and return the remaining material to your reference files. Be sure to take a few minutes to throw out any excess papers at this point, instead of saying, "I've got to clean that file out someday." It is much quicker and easier to do while the information is fresh in your remind.

**You can have an Action File and a Reference File with the same or similar file headings.**

For example, you might have a reference file entitled "Community Association" and an action file entitled "Community Association—Dues Campaign."

## When Action Is Too Packed

Clients with great piles of paper on their desks will frequently say, "I need all of this on my desk because I am working on it." But often a close look will determine that even though all the papers on the desk might need to be saved (although that's not always true, either!), not all of them are necessary to complete the particular project. A bulky action file often indicates that some of those papers could go in a reference file, or you may need two or more action files for one project, such as "Party—Menus" and "Party—Invitations."

If you lead a very simple lifestyle you may find that one file called "Action" is all you need, but for many people a pile of papers that need action would soon topple over. When the pile gets that deep, it is difficult to do anything. It soon takes as much time to find a project as it does to do it. When that situation exists, a major issue is decision-making.

## The Next Step

**R**emember that clutter is symptomatic of post-poned decisions. To simplify the decision-making process, it is helpful to recognize that the papers we need to take action on fall into categories. To determine the categories into which a particular piece of paper falls, ask yourself the question, "What is the *next* action I need to take on this piece of paper?" It is crucial that you recognize the significance of the word *next* in this question. The answer will tell you into which action file to put the paper. There are several possible answers to the question, and each answer is an action file category.

Sometimes it takes time to find the answer. For example, you have received a letter from Joe with question about membership in an association to which you belong. Your initial reaction may be, "I have to call Joe," but you realize you need to speak with Nancy first. And you can't talk intelligently to her until you have read the association's bylaws.

Joe's letter requires three actions: read the bylaws; call Nancy; and call Joe. You would therefore first put the letter in your "Call" action file with a temporary note on it to "Call Nancy" and "Call Joe." Then make an appointment with yourself (noted in your calendar) to "Read bylaws." Add **"C-Nancy/C-Joe"** to the note as a reminder that you're reading the bylaws to get information you can discuss in a call to Nancy before you call Joe.

## Potential Categories for Files

**H**ere are descriptions of a number of categories for action. Don't be intimidated by the number of categories; you probably won't need them all—and you might decide you need others that aren't described. Note in the margin categories you think you can use.

If, as you read through the listing, the whole idea begins to seem overwhelming, choose a few categories that particularly appeal to you and try them. If you're anything like the thousands of people who have adopted the system, you'll soon *love* it and wonder how you ever managed without it.

### Call

Many times the next action required on a piece of paper is a telephone call to someone. In addition to putting the paper in the "Call" file, you may wish to make a note on your calendar on the day you need to make the call. Using a symbol such as **"C"** will remind you that there is additional information in the "Call" file.

### Calls waiting

How many times have you received a telephone call in which the conversation began, "Hello. This is Anne Smith. I am returning your call." The knot in the pit of your stomach tightens as you frantically try to remember why you called her—or even who she is! If you have a note in your "Calls Waiting" file that tells you why you have left a message for that person to return your call, it can be a real stress-saver.

In addition, you can review the file periodically to check the current status of the calls. Were you simply returning their call, and the ball is now in their court, or do you really want to talk to them? If the former, after a period of time throw the paper out. If the latter, take the paper out of "Calls Waiting" and put it in "Call," with a note on your calendar to make the call again.

---

**Your Action Files**

As you read my descriptions of possible action files on pages 61–66, use the checklist below to note the ones you can use—and add your own.

☐ Call
☐ Calls Waiting
☐ Computer Entry
☐ Discuss
☐ File
☐ Hold for future
☐ Pay
☐ Photocopy
☐ Project
☐ Read
☐ Sign
☐ Special events
☐ Take to office/home
☐ Upcoming meetings/trips
☐ Write (Could divide into personal/business)
_____
_____
_____

## Computer entry

Some of the papers on your desk contain information that needs to be entered into your computer. It will be more time effective to make several entries at the same time—or delegate it to someone else to enter. When you've entered the material from this file into the computer, either throw out the papers, pass them on to someone else who may need them, or if you must save them, move them to the appropriate reference file.

Why, you may ask, if I'm helping you tame your paper tiger, would I suggest you keep paper after you've entered the information in your computer? The simple answer is that there are instances when you need to keep the paper. For example, you might track your investments on a computer, but you still need records of transactions for tax purposes. Be very careful what you do keep; it's all too easy to enter information and keep the paper anyway, "just in case." Ask yourself, "What's the worst thing that could happen if I don't have this paper? Can you live with the consequence? If so, toss; if not, file.

## Discuss

Communication is a major factor in managing the paper in our lives. Frequently we cannot take action on a matter until we have discussed it with another person. All of us have certain people in our lives with whom we routinely discuss issues, whether it is a spouse, a child, a colleague or a friend, or a professional resource. The "Discuss" category will contain several subcategories. For example, "Discuss—Mary," "Discuss—Accountant."

## File

People dislike filing and will put it off as long as possible. Even if you don't mind filing, but the file cabinet is in another room, you will need a "File" for those pieces of paper that need to go into the reference files. Many of the pieces of paper that arrive in the mail can go directly into "File" and never clutter the top of your desk. (For more information, see Chapter 11.)

## Hold for future

Many names have been applied to this category—suspension, tickler or pending are some examples. This is not a place to put papers that require action from you at this time. Rather, it is for papers that will require action at some future date, or that will require action after you have received additional information.

When you are tempted to put a piece of paper in this category because you are not certain of your decision, ask yourself, "What am I going to know tomorrow that I don't know today?" If the answer is "Nothing," you will know that you need to look further into the issue to find out what other category the paper really belongs in.

If you simply cannot make a decision at this time and you want to postpone the decision, put the paper in "Hold," but make a note on your calendar to remind you to consider the issue again. If you receive an invitation to dinner and with the invitation are the directions for getting to the host's home, put the invitation in "Hold for Future" with a symbol such as **"H"** beside the engagement notation on your calendar.

## Pay

This is the category to put all the bills you need to pay, as well as any other paper that requires writing a check—an order you wish to place or a donation you would like to make. If your household finances are quite complicated, you may wish to subdivide this category. For example, you could have a "Must Pay" for mortgage, utilities and car payment and a "Would Like to Pay" for potential donations, orders, subscriptions. If you pay some of the bills and your spouse pays others, you may wish to subdivide the category into "Pay—Betty" and "Pay—Bob." This is also a good place to put payment coupon books and reminders of deductions that are automatically taken from your checking account.

## Photocopy

Many times you cannot take the next action on a piece of paper until you get a photocopy. Such is fre-

**Action Notes**

quently the case in submitting medical insurance claims. Or you want to send a clipping from the local newspaper to your sister, but you also want a copy for yourself.

**Projects**

If you have several small projects going at once, you could keep the information for all of them in one file or you might prefer to keep a separate file for each one. Those projects that are currently active fall into the action-file category while those that are completed or have been put "on hold" temporarily go into the reference-file category.

If the project involves many papers, it may be appropriate to have a reference file and an action file. The action file would contain only those papers you need to complete the current step of the project. When that step is completed, review the materials in the file, discard what you don't need and return the rest to the reference file. Then move the papers relating to the next step of the project to the action file. "Project" files should be arranged alphabetically.

**Signature**

Sign several documents at once.

**Special events**

If you enjoy many outings—concerts, lectures, sports events—but have difficulty keeping track of them, you may wish to keep a separate "Events Calendar." When you receive a notice of an upcoming event, list it on your events calendar. Be sure, of course, to put definite commitments on your master calendar. Other options are to have a folder labeled "Schedules" in which you put these notices, or to hang them on the bulletin board. Then if you have a free evening you can check the folder to see what options you have. This is particularly helpful if you have out-of-town guests and you are assisting them in planning their schedules or you want to entertain them.

## Take to office/home

Designate a particular place to put those papers (and other items) you need to take with you to work. Choose a convenient location—on a table near the door, for example. Try keeping your briefcase at the same spot so that you can put things right into the briefcase. If your briefcase is not in the usual spot, put the item where your briefcase *should* be. Then when you return the briefcase it will be easy to get them together. This will stop the frustrating game of having one and not the other, and vice versa.

Have a similar setup in your office.

## Upcoming meetings/trips

Virtually every time you plan to go to a meeting or take a trip you will accumulate papers related to that event, whether it is an airplane ticket, a meeting agenda or a note from a friend asking you to call or visit when you are in the city.

When the trip or meeting is over, throw away those pieces of paper that are no longer essential and file the remaining papers according to how you will use them next. For example, the letter from your friend might contain an address that could be entered in your phone listing and then the letter could be tossed. Or you may wish to put the letter in your "Mementos" box to read again in the years to come. (See Chapter 18.)

## Write

Many times the next action you need to take on a piece of paper is writing a letter. "Write" includes business letters, personal letters, thank you notes and special occasion cards.

If writing is a problem area for you, take some time to think about what you can do to make the task easier. Many people find it helps to physically separate these categories. Sometimes you may feel like spending ten minutes writing a thank you note but not an hour writing an old college roommate. If you have to dig through a

*Ask yourself, "What is the next action I need to take on this piece of paper?"*

huge pile to find what interests you at the moment, you may lose interest before you find it!

I use airport waiting time to shop for greeting cards I like. Because I keep a supply of favorites on hand, sending a congratulations card literally takes only minutes—and I'm sure doing it makes me feel every bit as good as the person to whom I send it!

Keep postcards on hand for quick notes. Many people are now writing responses on the bottom of business letters and returning them to the sender to speed up response time. If you need a copy, put the paper in "Photocopy" or "Take to Office."

If you are procrastinating about writing a letter, ask yourself if a phone call would suffice, or at least get the process started. Or write an outline for yourself to help organize your thoughts and make the letter less difficult to write.

The major advantage to this system of file categories is an increased ability to manage your time effectively. It is a good time-management practice to group like activities together. Then, when you have ten minutes before a business meeting at work or before you need to meet your child at school, a quick look in "Call" can help you use those ten minutes to your advantage. Or if you're going to an appointment where you may have to wait, take along "Write" with some stationery for personal notes or some scratch paper to draft more formal correspondence.

## Logistics Strategy

You may well be feeling quite overwhelmed at this point! Anything new can seem overwhelming, so don't despair too early in the game. One question you may have is "Where do I put all these files?" Start with a series of manila file folders. You can put them in the front of the filing drawer in your desk, if there is one, in a stand-up rack on the top of your desk, or in a series of stack trays on your desk. Some people, who are afraid of the "out of sight out of mind" trap, keep the folders in a series of categorized piles on or near their desk.

As you experiment with the system, you will discover that each category does not have to be a "file" per se; nor does it have to be on your desk. For example, I know of no one whose "Read" category will fit into a file folder, and most people don't read at their work area. So "Read" could be in a basket beside your easy chair or the bed, or even in the bathroom—or, most likely, a combination. (See Chapter 15 for more detailed information on "Read.") You may want to keep "Photocopy" in a folder near the door or in your briefcase so you will have it when you go out.

## *All Those Files!*

**A**nother question you may have is "How do I remember to look in all those files?" Try it! You can put a symbol on your calendar to remind you to look. In many instances, such as "Call," there will undoubtedly be one call you will automatically remember to make. When you check the file for information on that call, you will be reminded of the others you want to make.

You may be confused with the similarity of the categories for the "To Do" list (Chapter 8) and the action files. Sometimes your "To Do" is just a thought, in which case you write it in your "To Do" book (or on a piece of paper in your action file). Other times, the "To Do" involves a piece of paper that goes in the action file. It is not a duplication, unless you choose to use a duplication system as an insurance policy.

CHAPTER

ELEVEN

# Your Reference Files

*The major reason
people procrastinate
about filing is that
they don't like making
the decision about
where the paper
should be filed.*

The reason for creating reference files is not just to be able to put papers away but it's also to be able to find them again! Research shows that 80% of the papers in most files are never used. So before you even begin to think about where you should file any piece of paper, think seriously about whether you should file it at all.

If you have a filing system that is not working or if you inherited someone else's system, read this chapter and start over. Don't try to fix the existing files. Instead, incorporate the information from the old system into the new system as you need it.

The components of an effective reference file are:

**Management**
**Mechanics**
**Maintenance**

In my work with clients, I frequently discover that two of these three factors are already in operation. As soon as the third factor is taken into account, their system starts to work.

## *File Management*

After you have considered the other five possibilities for a piece of paper—Wastebasket, Calendar, "To

Do" List, Rotary Phone File/Phone Book, and Action Files—and have determined that you wish to save this information for future use in your reference files, you need to decide how you will find it when you want it.

## Fear of Filing

One of the reasons people resist filing papers away is a fear that they will make a poor decision and file the paper in an inappropriate or hard-to-remember file. Here are some guidelines that will help you with your filing decisions:

**Ask yourself, "Under what circumstances would I want this information?"**

Be specific! "Just in case" will not help you find it again. If the answer is, "I might want this information if I were writing a speech," then the information should be saved in a "Speech Ideas" file. If you answer, "I will need this when I sell the house," then a "House—Main Street" file might be the answer.

**Ask yourself, "If I wanted this information, what word would first enter my mind?"**

The answer to that question will tell you what reference file is appropriate for this piece of paper. For example, a flyer about ordering candy from a specialty company could be filed under "Gift Ideas" or "Mail Order Information." And invitations from a past party could be filed under "Party Ideas," "Printing Ideas" or "Mementos."

**File information according to how you will use it, not where you got it.**

For example, your local homeowner's association published an article recommending repair services in the area. Suppose you wake up one morning to discover that you have no hot water for a shower. What are the chances you would remember that article in the "Homeowner's Association" file? A file labeled "Services—Household Repair" might be more useful.

*A file index is perhaps the most important step in managing your files.*

**Put all papers in their most general category first.**

For example, try keeping all of your warranties and instructions in a single file. Then, if the file becomes too bulky, break it down into "Warranties and Instructions—Appliances," "Warranties and Instructions—Clothing," etc.

It is easier to look through one file with 20 pieces of paper than 10 files with two papers in each; fewer places to look, fewer places to lose. The added advantage is that when you are using a file to get a particular piece of paper you remember you will also discover other pieces of paper you have forgotten. As a result you will be able to use more of the information you file.

**If a paper could be filed in more than one place, choose the one you are most likely to look in first.**

Write a note on the other file folders that says, "See also. . ." If you feel it is essential, make a copy for the second file.

**Organize your file consistently.**

For example, you may have medical and educational records for several members of the family. Decide whether you want all of John's files together; i.e., "John—Education," "John—Medical," or all medical files together, i.e., "Medical—Ann," "Medical—John."

**Group like files together.**

Whenever you have files you want to keep together physically in your file system, find a word that encompasses all the files. For example, instead of having a file that says "Biking" under "B" and "Skiing" under "S', you could have "Recreation—Biking" and "Recreation—Skiing."

*File Index*

A file index is the final and perhaps the most important step in managing your files. The same information can be filed several ways. For example, I could file information about my car in "Automobile," "Car," "Chrysler," or

"Vehicle." The problem comes if you file information under "Car" one time and under "Chrysler" the next—and your spouse looks for it under "Automobile!"

This dilemma can be avoided by making an alphabetical list of all file names, with cross references to files that contain related material. When you are writing or typing the index, leave space between each letter of the alphabet so you will have room to add new file titles as you need them. Put as many names on one page as possible; use columns if necessary. It's unlikely you'll ever get to the filing if you have to read a 15-page guide first! (See page 72 for an example of a file index. The categories shown are described on pages 73–77. Use this sample as your starting point by crossing out categories you won't need and adding in those you will.)

Keep your file index accessible in hard copy in the very front of your filing system or at your desk. Make changes with pen or pencil. Keep the list in your computer so you can update it quickly and easily. When you read an article you want to file, check the index to see what file already exists that might be appropriate for that particular article.

Use the index if you are looking for an article. It is much easier to check a file index to see where you might find an article than it is to open the file drawer and go through file after file.

The index is particularly important if you are learning a new system or if more than one person will be using the same system. Keep in mind also that if there is a particular piece of paper you are afraid of losing, you can list it on the index. For example, "Birth Certificate"—See "Legal Information."

### Sample Headings for Your System

You may wish to organize your files into various categories. A friend of mine divides her files into three categories: Financial and legal, reference, and children. Some people put all files that involve payments of any kind into one category and all other files in a reference category.

## Sample Reference File Index

Art Owned

Articles

_____

_____

_____

Book Information

_____

_____

Car Maintenance

Childcare

Church/Synagogue

Consumer Information

Credit Cards

_____

_____

_____

Death Information

Diet

_____

_____

_____

Entertainment

Education Records

_____

_____

Financial Records

_____

_____

_____

_____

Gardening/Plants

Gift Ideas

_____

_____

Hobbies

Holidays

Home Decorating

Household Maintenance

Humor

_____

Income Tax

Insurance—Car

Insurance—Household

Insurance—Life

Insurance—Medical

   Bills to be submitted

   Bills submitted-not paid

   Bills paid

Inventory

IRA

_____

_____

Maps/Directions

_____

_____

Party Records

Personal Property

_____

_____

_____

Quotes

_____

Recreation

Resume

Retirement

_____

_____

_____

Safe Deposit Box

Services

Shopping

Special Interests

Subscriptions/Memberships

Stocks

_____

_____

_____

_____

Travel

_____

_____

_____

_____

Warranties

_____

_____

_____

Be aware that there are always gray areas when you begin categorizing. For example, you might think of "Medical" as a reference file or a financial file. You can eliminate the problem of determining what category a file should be in by filing everything strictly by the alphabet. Then if you are looking for "Medical," there is no question of where to look.

Keep in mind also that your filing system will change as your life circumstances change. For example, if you get married you will need to decide whether to maintain two separate filing systems or combine them into one. If you decide to combine them, you may want to use color to identify files that belong specifically to one person. (But color coding can also cause problems, as discussed later in this chapter.)

The following is a list of the kinds of information that can be put in a home filing-system. Detailed information about what could go into the files can be found in the chapters in Part 2, "Strategies for Paper Management." The categories are listed here alphabetically, as you would file them. As you read about categories you could use—and think of others that are not listed here—jot them down in the sample file index on the opposite page.

**Art Owned**

Could also be filed under "Personal Property" or "Insurance."

**Articles**

This could be divided into categories by subject, e.g. "Articles—Psychology"

**Book Information**

This could be divided into categories such as "Books—Novels," "Books—History" etc.

**Car Maintenance**

Keep copies of all receipts from work done on your car, along with the manual that came with the car when you bought it. Information could also be filed under "Automobile" or "Ford."

### Childcare Information
Include summer camp information and photocopies of blank forms to be filled out with information for the sitter. Information could also be filed under "Babysitter" or "Camp."

### Church/Synagogue
This could be listed under specific name: "Calvary Church," "Temple Zion," for example.

### Consumer Information
If this file becomes too bulky, divide it into categories such as "Consumer Information—Electronics," Consumer Information—Real Estate," etc.

### Credit Cards
For each account, enter card number, address, and phone number to call if card is lost. (Keep a duplicate copy of the list in your safe deposit box.)

### Death Information
What to do in case of your death or a relative's. Include a copy of wills. (Originals should go in the safe deposit box.)

### Diet Information
This could also be placed under "Health" or "Nutrition."

### Entertainment
Put ideas for outings for family or house guests. This could be divided into categories.

### Education Records
Make one file for each member of family.

**Financial Records**

Separate general financial planning information from your personal information. This file could contain information about loans, mortgages, investments, etc.

**Gardening and Plants**

**Gift Ideas**

**Hobbies**

Divide into specific areas such as "Gardening," "Coins," etc.

**Holidays**

File here ideas for gifts, record of gifts given, ideas for next year, if you send one, copies of your annual letter you send to friends and family, etc.

**Home Decorating**

Divide into specific areas if too bulky for one file.

**Household Maintenance Records**

**Humor**

Favorite cartoons, jokes, articles.

**Income Tax Information**

Divide this file into subfiles for each tax year. Keep all records you may need in case of an audit. These include records of donations, taxes paid, receipts for any tax deductible items. (See Chapter 14 for information on how long you need to keep these records.)

**Insurance**

You will need several files for this important category. Keep one for "Car," another for "Household/Personal Property" (including receipts for art, jewelry, furs, etc.), a third for "Life Insurance" and a fourth for "Medical Insurance," which in turn should be broken

*Date information when you file it so it will be easy to tell if it's recent enough to be useful.*

down into 3 folders—"Bills to Be Submitted" (keep blank forms here), "Bills Submitted But Not Paid," and "Bills Paid"

**Inventory**
List items in various storage areas of your home or in other locations.

**IRA**
This information could be included in "Retirement Information," or perhaps with "Financial Records."

**Maps and Instructions**
Directions to friends' homes, photocopies of map to your home.

**Party Records**
Guest lists, menus of past parties and ideas for future ones.

**Personal Property**
Specifics on valuable items owned, if not already in Insurance file.

**Quotes and Favorite Articles**
This could also be called "Speech Ideas" if you make frequent public appearances.

**Recreation**
This file can be divided into various sports and activities.

**Resume**

**Retirement Information**
Keep your latest pension statement here. If you're enrolled in other pension plans from former employers, also keep information on those accounts here. IRA and Keogh statements could be filed here as well.

**Safe Deposit Box**

Keep a list of what is located there. Also use this file for temporary storage of items to take to your safe deposit box.

**Services**

This file could be divided into "Personal" and "Household") for information such as hair stylist, physical therapist, plumber, electrician, etc.

**Shopping Information**

Mail order information, clippings about new stores, and brochures are filed here.

**Special Interests**

Divide this file into categories such as "History," "Psychology."

**Subscriptions and Memberships**

Keep records of renewals and order forms here.

**Stocks, Bonds and Mutual Funds**

Divide into separate subfiles for each investment you own. Keep broker statements here, along with annual reports. Also make a separate file here for information on stocks, bonds or mutual funds you're considering buying.

**Travel**

If you have a lot of information here, divide the file into geographic areas.

**Warranties and Instructions**

Divide this file into types, e.g., "Major Appliances," "Lawn Tools," or "Home Electronics."


## *File Mechanics*

The importance of the mechanics of a filing system is frequently overlooked. Very few people enjoy filing;

most people dislike it intensely! There are three major reasons: They dislike deciding where to file the papers; they dislike the physical discomfort of jamming hands into overstuffed file drawers; or they dislike the annoyance of looking into numerous file drawers before they find the file they need.

### Your Choice of a File Cabinet

Choosing your file cabinet is an important decision. My first choice, without a doubt, is a good-quality full-suspension file cabinet. Full suspension means that you can open the drawers all the way so that no files are obstructed from view.

There are two types of file cabinets, vertical and lateral, which are distinguished by how they open. Vertical cabinets are generally 28″ high, 15″ wide and 26″ deep. The drawer pulls out the full depth of the cabinet, and files are arranged from front to back. Lateral file cabinets are generally 28″ high and 18″ deep and come in widths of 30″, 36″, or 42″. The depth is approximately 35″ when the drawer is open, and the files can be arranged front to back in rows or side to side. Any good office supply store will have a catalog in which you can see pictures of the various options, even if they do not have them in stock.

Decide whether to purchase letter- or legal-size files. Unless your life is complicated with many legal issues and you have a substantial amount of legal-sized paper, I would recommend letter size. You will take up less space and save a significant amount of money on the cost of the file folders.

For most households a two-drawer, full-suspension vertical cabinet will be enough. If you want to create additional working space in your work area, a good choice would be a two-drawer full-suspension lateral file. If you want or need more filing space, you can purchase a four- or five-drawer file.

You can find less expensive file cabinets at a discount store, but I do not recommend them for files you use frequently. If you cannot afford a full-suspension file, you may find that filing boxes are more accessible than a poorly made metal cabinet. Keep in mind that a good quality file cabinet is a lifetime investment. Prices vary dramatically, so after you have found the cabinet you want compare prices.

If you don't have room for a traditional filing cabinet or you feel it does not fit with your interior decor, there are other options ranging from cardboard or plastic file boxes to solid wood cabinets designed to match your furniture. Portable file folders work well if you use your kitchen or dining room table as a work space and want to move the files with you when you work. They also work well for files that you need access to only occasionally, and that you store in the basement, attic, garage or some other out-of-the-way place.

## Your Choice of File Folders

One of the major decisions to make in setting up a filing system is what kind of file folders you will use. There are multiple options.

"Hanging Files" are my preference. Although they are more expensive than manila folders, they will last significantly longer, and the plastic stand-up tabs make the labels much easier to read.

If your filing cabinet does not accommodate hanging files, you can purchase a hanging-file frame that can be sized to fit your file drawer.

It is not necessary to put manila file-folders inside the hanging files, but there are a few situations when that is advisable to do so. You may sometimes need to take material away from home or office to use it. For example, you could use a manila folder to keep a file for a committee on which you serve so you can take the information in the folder with you to the meeting. If you do use two folders, label the hanging file and the manila file identically. This will make it easy to return the file to its proper place.

You could also use manila folders within a hanging file when you need to make subdivisions in the file. For example, the hanging folder could be labeled "Car," and

**Put labels on the front of folders. When you file a paper and grab the plastic tab the file automatically opens to the place you need to file the paper.**

the manila folders could be labeled "Car Insurance," "Car Repairs," etc.

If you are using manila files, crease the fold lines at the bottom of the folder to increase the capacity of the folder and prevent obstruction of the file label. There are special files called "Interior Files" that are slightly shorter than regular manila folders so there is no risk of the tabs obstructing the view of the plastic tabs on the hanging file.

Another type of file is the "Box-Bottom" files, which are useful for very thick files, or a file that has many subdivisions. These have a one-half to three-inch cardboard strip in the bottom.

Hanging folders come in a variety of colors, as do other types of file folders. The hanging folders sometimes come with colored plastic tabs, but in the case of the darker colors, such as red and blue, you may prefer to substitute clear plastic labels that are easier to read, particularly if you used typed labels.

Plastic tabs can go on the front or back of hanging files. Most people put them on the back, probably because it is consistent with the label on the back of manila folders. Try putting them on the front instead. The big advantage of having the label on the front is that when you are filing a piece of paper and you grab the plastic tab the file automatically opens to the place you need to file the paper. Use whichever method you prefer, but be consistent.

There are also many other kinds of file folders available. If you have no filing cabinet but have shelf space, use file folders with labels on the narrow end instead of on the top. Then you can put your files on shelves and still see the labels easily.

Some people like to use file folders with metal fasteners so that the papers can be punched and put in the file in chronological order and will stay that way. In most instances I find that the results are not worth the effort. Over and over again, I have seen filing pile up because it took too much time and effort to get the holes punched.

### Able Labels

Labeling is the key to an effective filing system. Often I find files with penciled labels—or no label at all because they are only "temporary" files. But many files become like the "temporary" building on my college campus that served as the music building for 27 years! It is very simple to use peel-off file labels so that if you need to change the label you can do so easily. In the meantime, you have a file you can easily find.

Determine what the label should say by asking the question: "If I wanted this information again what word would I think of?" as previously discussed in "File Management."

Type labels only if a typewriter is always available and you are comfortable enough with the typewriter to be able to do it easily or have someone do it for you. Even though I am a proficient typist, and have a secretary, I still prefer to handwrite file labels because they are easier to read. I find that printing labels in capital letters creates the most consistent, readable appearance. Use a dark-colored felt-tipped pen of medium thickness, and make sure to print clearly so that others can read the headings. One client attaches a pen on a string inside the file cabinet so the pen is always there when she wants it.

Some people like to color-code their files, and there are lots of ways to do so. You could use colored file folders, colored file labels, colored dots to stick on labels, or colored pens to write labels. Color is very useful if it tells a story. For example, you could use red labels on any files that contain information you will need at tax time, or you could use a different color for each member of the family.

But color can also be confusing if it's not used consistently and very frustrating when you want to make a file quickly but can't find the right color label, pen or dot. I would caution you to use color sparingly unless you have someone to help you with the file mechanics or you particularly enjoy doing it yourself.

Whatever type of file folder you choose, put the key

**Handwritten labels are easier to read.**

word at the left of the label when writing or typing labels. For example, "Education—John—1992" rather than "1992—Education—John." And beware of the "Just for now" trap! Keep the system simple enough so that you can maintain it as you go.

## Too Many Systems

One of the temptations—and most frequent mistakes—in setting up a filing system is to create too many systems. In doing this you create more work for yourself. If you are looking for information, you first have to remember which filing system it is in and then determine where it is in the system. If you are trying to file information, you may find it difficult to determine which system is appropriate for that information. Unless there is a clear-cut identity, such as all files involving financial information, keep all files together in one A-Z system. Then if you are looking for "Entertaining," you will go directly to "E," instead of wondering whether you put it in the "personal" files or the "house" files.

## Special Mechanics Tips

The following are additional tips that will make the mechanics of your filing easier.

### Avoid using paper clips in files.

They take up more space and, more importantly, catch on papers when you file them, obstructing the file label. Instead, use staples to keep together papers that are related. Also keep a staple remover handy.

### File papers with the most recent on the top.

When you open the file you can immediately see the latest action or information. This will also make cleaning the file take less time because the oldest information will automatically be on the bottom.

### Arrange the file folders alphabetically.

If you have resisted this idea in the past, try it. You will be surprised at how much more quickly you will be able to find the file you are looking for.

**Label the outside of the file cabinet as to its contents, either by subject or by alphabet.**

This will save you opening the third drawer when the file you want is in the second.

## File Maintenance

**N**o matter how much time and energy you spend creating a system to fit your particular needs, you will still need to adopt a plan to maintain the system. The following steps will help.

**Determine when—or if—you will do the filing.**

More and more professional people are recognizing that it is cost effective to hire someone else to do the routine household management tasks—including filing—just as we hire others to maintain the lawn.

If you will be doing your own filing, decide how you will keep the "File" pile from becoming larger than the file cabinet. Some people file when they pay bills. That way, two potentially unpleasant tasks are done at the same time, and they can reward themselves with a more pleasant activity when they're finished. Other people wait until the "File" tray is full.

The major reason people procrastinate about filing is that they don't like making the decision about where the paper should be filed. That decision is easier to make when you have just read the letter or article. Remember that if you circle the key word or write it in the upper right hand corner before you put the paper in the "To File" tray or your "File" action file, the filing task will be only a mechanical one and will take less time.

This method is essential if someone else does your filing because no two people would necessarily put a paper in the same file. A paper relating to your car insurance, for example, could be filed under "Car" or "Insurance." In this instance, the File Index again becomes invaluable.

*It's easier to look through one file with 20 pieces of paper than 10 files with two pieces each.*

**Action Notes**

**Clean out files as you use them.**

I cannot count how many times I have seen clients with a paper in hand they knew could be tossed say, "I'll have to clean this out someday," and promptly put the piece of paper back into the file again instead of directly into the wastebasket!

**Establish an annual "File Clean-Out Day."**

Around tax time is frequently a good time, since you will be looking into many of your files at that time anyway. An alternative is to wait until you need the file space. As long as you have room to file papers easily the issue of purging is not a major one. But when you neglect filing the paper you would like to file because it is physically uncomfortable or downright impossible to get your fingers into the file cabinet, then the time for Clean Out Day has arrived!

*How Long Is Enough?*

Determine how long you need to keep the papers you file. Date information when you file it so it will be easy to tell if it is recent enough to be useful. In certain cases, such as a file of newsletters, you can put the retention information right on the file label. For example, "Community Newsletter—Keep one year."

The issue of retention guidelines is a difficult one. In many instances the decision is purely discretionary. How long do you want to keep articles you intend to read or reviews of restaurants? In other cases, you should simply keep material forever, updating the information as necessary. This would include birth certificates, wills, insurance policies, school and medical records, etc.

There are legal reasons for keeping other material for a certain amount of time. This material mostly deals with financial and tax matters. For quick reference to see how long you should keep what, turn to the chart in the Appendix.

There are other factors to consider in making your decision about retaining material. One is space. If you have enough of it (say a basement) to keep everything—

and it doesn't make you feel uncomfortable to have that paper laying around—then ignore it. Be sure the material is well organized—and make sure to separate the "archival materials" from those you are currently using.

But even if you have ample room for storage, if you get a knot in your stomach every time you open the file drawer or closet door, the price you are paying for your failure to make decisions about paper retention is high, and you should look for alternatives.

P A R T

T W O

# Strategies for Paper Management

# Papers for Proof, Pleasure and Pondering

Every piece of paper in your life can be managed by using the techniques described in the previous seven chapters. However, there are several categories of papers that particularly plague many households.

There are essential papers relating to paying taxes and bills and for keeping family records. And there are other kinds of paper that seem to multiply like mushrooms in various places around the house—maps, coupons, flyers from local businesses, and instruction books that come with new electronic gadgets, kitchen appliances and garden tools.

Activities create more paper—travel, family celebrations, seminars, recreation and sports events. Medical emergencies, education pursuits, career changes, job responsibilities, religious affiliations, club memberships, and community involvement add still more paper.

Contributing to the accumulation are photographs and other family mementos, recipes, books, and articles from magazines and newspapers to which you want to refer in the future.

And let's not forget about the papers relating to your children—papers that you need to keep about them, papers they need to keep relating to the management of their own lives, and still more papers you or

*Give yourself enough time to develop new habits for handling paper efficiently.*

they want to save as memories of their achievements.

You will undoubtedly have questions about certain pieces of paper and will discover a variety of ways you could handle them. How do you know which is best?

## No Right or Wrong Way

Remember, there is no "right" or "wrong" way to organize anything. If you asked three different interior designers to redesign your living room, you would obviously get three different results. You might like all three of the plans, but probably one of them would appeal to you more than the others. If you asked three different people to write a newspaper article about a community event, you would undoubtedly get three different stories. They would probably all be accurate but would be colored by the personal experiences and views of the individual authors.

Paper management has this same variety and flexibility. The next 11 chapters will discuss some of the major areas of paper management that you will have to face in your life. You will find different approaches for handling these challenges, along with some of the pros and cons for each method. Choose the way that sounds the most feasible to you. Be sure to give it a fair try.

Many people fail in setting up new systems because they do not allow enough time to develop the new habits that are necessary to make any kind of change in their life. Try the new system for a reasonable amount of time—two to three months is usually adequate. If the new system is still not working, ask yourself these questions: "Is the problem that I don't have enough time? If so, what can I do to make the time?" "Am I having problems with the mechanics? If so, who can help me?" "Do I really want to do this? If not, is there anyone else who can do it? Or, what would happen if I didn't do it? What would I do then?"

Often, all that is required for success is a modification of the system. Spend some time identifying what you liked about the system you tried and what you did not. With that information, you can move on to make the necessary changes to create a system that will work for you.

## Who's in Charge Here?

One of the questions that inevitably arises in every household is *who* is going to manage the paper? Answering this question can create a major conflict if there is no one in the family who is willing to do it, or if there is a disagreement about how the paper should be handled.

Communication and negotiation are the keys to success in family paper management. In most households, specific responsibilities are assigned to specific people. One person may pay bills, while another does the filing. Or, a husband and wife may elect to pick a "bill-paying night" and do it together.

If one person generally does the filing, other family members should know something about the system in case that person is ill or absent. If one person tears out a newspaper article for filing, that same person should identify where to file it if he or she expects to be able to find it again. (See Chapter 11 for more details on this subject.) In fact, every member of the household will have some papers to handle. Children need to learn to take care of their own papers to help them learn to be independent.

If one family member is more skilled in paper management—or more willing to learn—the entire family will benefit. In that case, the paper manager should be excused from doing some other household chores such as shopping errands, household maintenance or outdoor maintenance.

As it is with any attempt at learning something new, you will discover stumbling blocks. Don't let that stop you! In every organizing process, things will seem worse before they get better. A natural outcome of sorting through piles of papers is a renewed awareness that we

*A natural outcome of sorting through piles of papers is a renewed awareness that we are not as productive as we would like to be.*

are not as productive as we would like to be. Concentrate on how you are going to improve the situation now, not what you should have done in the past.

## How Does it Make You Feel?

Sometimes my clients have a great deal of difficulty letting go of the excess in their lives, whether it is paper, clothes, kitchen utensils or their children's outgrown toys. If that is true in your case, ask the question, "How does having this make me feel?" If the answer is anything negative—sad, angry, guilty—then decide whether you want to continue to surround yourself with anything that makes you feel unhappy.

The clarity of our goals and our willingness to look at the future instead of dwelling on the past is another important factor in our ability to make decisions about what we need to keep. If you find yourself unable to make progress with letting go of things you know deep down inside you really don't need, it might be one symptom of a deeper underlying problem. You may even wish to seek professional help in setting some specific goals in your life.

# THIRTEEN

# Bills, Bills, Bills

**W**e are able to laugh about many of the papers in our lives, but there is little humor in unpaid bills. A lost bill can mean a disconnected telephone or a cold house in December. Bills can represent emotionally charged issues such as the extravagant new suit that you've never worn or the vacation that fizzled.

We must not only deal with the issue of finding the money to pay bills, but we must also determine who

*It is not necessary to open a bill at the time you receive it.*

Disorganized Bills

Organized Bills

It Pays To Keep Track of Your Bills.

**In the interest of financial planning, it is wiser to pay bills once a month.**

pays them—when, where, and how. Frequently clients spend more time debating whether to postpone paying a bill than it would have taken for them to write the check. And how embarrassing it is when the mortgage company calls about your delinquent payment and you can't even find the payment book!

## Keeping Track

**O**ne of the major factors in reducing the stress of paying bills is establishing a method to keep track of them. The simplest method is to put all the bills in one place, pay them at least once a month, and then file all the receipts in one place, or in different places depending on the type of expense involved. If you need to refer to the payment, you will be able to find the information.

Using this method, note that it is not necessary to open a bill at the time you receive it. In fact, unless you plan to do something specific with the information in the bill at that time, I don't particularly recommend it. The result of just opening many bills without acting on them is a significant increase in the number of pieces of paper you have to handle. More importantly, you increase the likelihood that the bill and its return envelope will get separated.

If you're not going to pay all the bills at one time, you need a good method to keep track of when to pay them. Try opening them and marking the amount due and the due date on the front of the envelope. Then put a note on your calendar on the day you need to pay the bill. Still another method is to make a list of the bills as they come in. Then you can check them off as you pay them, noting the date paid and the check number. This list can be useful for future reference.

Many people keep track of their expenses. This book is not intended to be a financial-planning guide; there are several good resources on that subject at your local bookstore or library. The issue of tracking expenses as it relates to paper management, however, has to do with when you will record your expenses. Decide whether you will enter the information in your budget book when you pay bills or if that is an unrealistic expectation for one sitting. If it is, determine when you will enter your expenses, just as you determined when you would pay your bills. Make an appointment with yourself and mark it in your calendar until you're in the habit of recording the information.

## Time to Pay Up

A key element in creating a bill-paying system that works for you is recognizing that it must be done—by someone. If you hate doing it, do not assume that *you* have to be that someone. Your spouse might not mind handling the job. Many financial institutions offer a direct-payment service. Find out if any offer a bill-payer system that allows you to pay your bills by punching the amounts into your touchtone telephone. There are also computer programs designed to pay bills electronically. And more and more people are hiring others to do tasks like bill-paying so that they have time and energy for other activities that are more fun—and maybe profitable, thus providing funds to pay for the service.

If, however, you do not have the luxury of someone to help you pay your bills, what can you do to make the task more palatable?

The first step is to determine the best time for you to pay bills. Do you prefer to pay them once or twice a month or to pay each one as it arrives?

In the interest of financial planning, it is wiser to pay bills once a month. This method gives you the opportunity to look at your overall financial picture and to make financial decisions based on hard facts, rather than on feelings and fears. For example, if you know you can't pay off the balance on all of your credit card bills, pay the one with the highest interest rate.

However, if you know yourself well enough to recognize that you will procrastinate on a task that

## Reduce Your Credit Cards

One way to reduce the paper in your life is to keep fewer credit cards. You'll also save on annual fees. And try to pay off credit card bills monthly so you don't pay non-deductible interest. If you must carry a balance, make sure your card has a low interest rate. And if you own a home, consider a home equity loan, the interest on which is most likely tax deductible.

feels overwhelming—that is, facing a mountain of bills all at once—you may be better off paying each bill as it comes in.

## A Place to Pay Up

**W**hatever method you decide to use, there are certain decisions you must make. If you pay your bills at home, choose where you will do it. If you are going to pay bills as they arrive, the location where you'll pay them must be convenient; otherwise it will be too much trouble to go there and you will not do it.

If you pay bills once or twice a month, it is essential that you have a convenient place to put your "Pay" action file so you can put bills in the folder as they come in and you're sorting the mail. This place doesn't have to be the same place where you will eventually pay the bills.

Be sure to have everything you need in your bill-paying location—stamps, envelopes, a pen that works, your checkbook, and a place to put the receipts from the paid bills. Have a large wastebasket within reach for all those flyers with the "too good to be true" temptations! Finally, be sure to get the stamped bills to a place where you will see them so they actually get to the mailbox. Frequently amid my clients' piles of papers, I find checks they wrote but never mailed. Failure to mail a payment can cause frustration and confusion when you receive a delinquency notice for a bill you thought you'd paid. Your check register indicates you paid it. You remember writing the check. Did it get lost in the mail? Did the company make a mistake? Only when your bank statement arrives, or you call the company, can you know for sure whether or not you paid the bill. And if it turns out you hadn't made the payment, you also have to pay past due penalties.

If you pay bills at the office, establish a system for getting the bills from your mailbox at home to the office. Put them in a basket near the door, in a file on your desk or directly into your briefcase. You can also arrange to have the bills mailed directly to your office.

## Statements: To Save or Not to Save

**A**fter you have paid the bills, then the question is, "What do I do with the statements?" To answer, ask yourself: "What is the reason I would need this statement?" If you recall your past habits, you may realize that you have indeed never used the information. You might then decide to throw the statements away, knowing that you can always refer to your canceled checks and check register.

One possibility is to keep a record of payments to a particular company in case there are billing questions. Put the statements in a reference file marked "Master Card," or "Sears," or a more generic file, "Bills Paid."

Another function of such a file could be to provide a record of personal expenses. For example, if you are divorced you may keep records of expenditures on children in case a problem develops with child support. If so, create a reference file called "Child Support," "Children," or "Financial Information—Children."

You may keep certain statements for specific, but temporary, circumstances. For example, if you are planning to sell your home within the next year, keep the utility bills because the information will interest a potential buyer.

Frequently the primary reason for keeping the information is "For the IRS." See the next chapter for detailed information.

Another area of concern related to bills is the credit card receipt—those flimsy little pieces of paper stuffed in the pockets of your suit, lying on top of your dresser and buried in your briefcase or desk drawers. What should you do with them? One simple method is to get several business-size envelopes—one for each credit card. Put the name of one card on each envelope and, if you have

*Try using a series of business-sized envelopes to store credit card receipts.*

the space, hang the envelopes on a bulletin board with the flap tucked inside to create a pocket. When you return home, put those receipts in the appropriate envelopes. When the credit card bills arrive, you can match them up with the receipts in minutes and pay the bills. (The envelope method also works well for bank statements.)

Keep in mind that you need to keep most of those receipts only until you see that the purchase or deposits have been recorded accurately on your statement. Some receipts must be retained for tax and other financial record-keeping purposes. Unless you want to keep the rest as records of a purchase, toss them!

# The Tax Man Cometh

**S**omeone once said that to live comfortably it's not how much you earn, but how much you keep after taxes. You might hate to pay them, think the system is unfair, dislike the forms, and stage a mini-tax rebellion, but in the end the tax man cometh—sometimes with penalty!

It's April 7. You haven't seen the top of the dining room in two weeks because shopping bags and shoe boxes of paid bills and receipts, piles of canceled checks

*A less than perfect recordkeeping system is better than no system at all.*

## It May Come As A Surprise . . .

Most taxpayers don't *really* have to file by April 15 because they don't owe a dime with their returns! There's no penalty for missing the deadline if you are due a refund. But don't wait too long! You still have to file a return; failing to do so until after the IRS figures you are late—and asks you about it—could mean a penalty.

and unidentified cash register receipts cover it. There are more receipts in the bottom of your briefcase, the back of the dresser drawer and on your kitchen counter.

To add to the chaos, there is the 15-page guide from your accountant with instructions on what information he or she needs. Heads pound and stomachs churn as the countdown begins to April 15. What can you do to minimize the stress around this deadline?

## Two Kinds of Taxpayers

First, it is important to recognize that there are basically two kinds of taxpayers—those who feel comfortable only if they record deductions as they occur during the year and those who prefer to ignore the entire issue until the fear of the penalty for late payment is greater than their willingness to procrastinate.

Somewhere in our education about managing our financial affairs we heard the message that the *right* way to keep tax records is on a daily, or at least some frequent, basis. We envision a professional-looking ledger with neat entries and accurate totals at the end of each month. Most of all we dream of walking into the tax accountant's office the first week of February with everything in order!

There are *many* ways to maintain tax information. One man I know files all his receipts in two huge garbage bags—one labeled "Tax Deductible" and the other "Non-Tax Deductible." He then ignores the issue of taxes until the deadline hovers over him and then digs in.

Most people require a slightly more sophisticated system. Some people require a *much* more sophisticated system. But everyone should have *some* system because the more records you have, the more claims you can prove—and the more money you will save. If your records are incomplete, you're likely to pay Uncle Sam more than you legally owe.

If you have never filed your taxes before April 15, you are probably not the type of person who will conscientiously maintain daily records. Perhaps you should accept that as a reality—and plan accordingly!

Determine your style of recordkeeping and weigh the alternatives for yourself. What are the risks of postponing the task? What is the worst possible thing that could happen? What would you do in that situation? Do you need an on-going system to feel secure? Is it reasonable to design a system that requires daily entries, or is it more realistic to accept the fact that you will not deal with taxes until April?

## Crucial Steps

Regardless of your style, there are certain steps that are crucial:

- If you have a tax advisor, make an appointment to get together well before April 15 to determine exactly what records you need to keep if it is not clear to you. This will eliminate unnecessary paper, and insure that you retain essential information.
- Designate a place to keep any information relevant to your tax return. It can be a dresser drawer, a file, a shoebox, a calendar, a computer—in short, anything that works for you
- Pay tax-deductible items by check or credit card whenever possible. At the end of the year, sorting canceled checks and credit card receipts is much easier than sorting cash register receipts with blurred dates and miscellaneous unidentified scraps of paper. Some banks and brokerage firms even offer systems that break out taxable items paid by check. Computer software programs are also available for that purpose.
- Ask yourself how much of your recordkeeping or tax preparation you really need or want to do yourself. Is there someone who can help—another family member, perhaps, or a professional?

## The On-Going System

In my experience, it is possible, and preferable, to avoid all the last-minute work if you can. What are the advantages of an on-going recordkeeping system?

*Pay tax-deductible items by check or credit card whenever possible. Sorting them is much easier than sorting cash register receipts with blurred dates or unidentified scraps of paper.*

*Your chances of defending deductions in case you're audited are greater if there is evidence that your expenses were noted "contemporaneously."*

A key advantage is that you are less likely to omit legitimate expenses if you record them as they occur. You will also be able to make better financial decisions, particularly if your income varies from month to month, as in the case of many self-employed people.

An on-going recordkeeping system also helps in case you're audited. Your chances of defending your deductions are greater if there is evidence that your expenses were noted "contemporaneously," as the IRS states it. Taxpayers are no longer permitted to re-create records months later to satisfy an audit, unless the records were destroyed in an extreme circumstance such as fire or flood.

If your return is audited, records are essential. Legitimate expenses may be disallowed for lack of documentation. If that is not enough to spur you into action, consider the high cost of interest and penalties on past due tax.

Finally, if you've kept accurate records through the year, you'll find it easier to get your information to your tax accountant or file your forms yourself before the April rush. One of my clients routinely used to request an extension on April 15 instead of filing his return. After we worked out a recordkeeping system, he was able to file his return early for the first time in his life, and he received a refund on March 15! Instead of paying a penalty for non-payment of taxes, he received an interest payment on his savings account.

If you choose to keep your records as you go, make an appointment with yourself to get it done, whether at the end of each working day, or at the time you pay the bills. If you record expenses on a calendar, choose one with enough space to write—or use a separate notebook. Don't let perfectionism defeat you. If you forget to record a luncheon expense at the time, decide what you can do next time. A less than perfect recordkeeping system is better than no system at all.

Keep accurate records of income from all sources—for example, your job, freelance work, and interest paid and capital gains realized from savings accounts and investments. Note the source of the income in your check register. IRS auditors frequently match deposit records to amounts declared on tax returns. If you cannot prove that a $2,000 deposit is repayment of a loan to a friend by showing a copy of your original check or other transmittal, the IRS could treat the entire amount as taxable income.

File records of deductible items such as medical bills, charitable donations or casualty losses as soon as you get them. The system that demands the least amount of work has two clearly labeled envelopes for each deductible category: expenses paid by check or credit card; cash receipts. The information in these envelopes will not be needed unless you are audited by the IRS and need additional supporting evidence.

## The April Approach

It is also possible, with certain preliminary precautions, to wait until April 15 is just around the corner and still do the job effectively. It makes little difference whether you spend ten minutes a day, one hour a week, or three days a year working on taxes. If waiting until the last minute is your normal approach, accept it and plan for it. Here's a game plan that should help you out.

Even if you prefer the April Approach for organizing your records, remember that you still have to have the records available when the time comes. First collect the records—canceled checks, credit card receipts and statements, bank statements, cash register receipts, calendars, and any articles or other information you may have collected about what you can deduct—and sort them.

When all the papers have been separated into the appropriate piles, place each category into a separate container, such as a large envelope, plastic basket, or shoe box. Label each category clearly. Since you will probably need more than one sitting to complete your taxes, these labeled containers make it easier to clear your work area, if necessary, and to find your place when you are ready to continue.

Now take one category at a time. Eliminate dupli-

*If you usually get a tax refund, the faster you file, the faster the money goes into your bank account to earn interest for you instead of the IRS.*

cate receipts; for example, keep either the customer copy of a credit card payment or the copy sent with your monthly statement. Always keep the receipt with the most complete information, or staple the receipts together. If you need to correlate your charges with your calendar in order to prove a tax deductible expense, such as in the case of entertainment, put all receipts in chronological order to speed up the process.

## Preparing to File

Whether you keep your papers organized through the year or you wait to organize them when you do your taxes, the rest of the process is the same. Use a calulator with a tape to total the receipts for each category of deductible item and staple the tape to each pile. Write the category on the tape. If you use an accountant, make an itemized list of your deductions so the accountant can double check your work, and so it will be easier to support your claim in the case of an audit.

While you've held most of the information concerning your deductions through the year, other records of deductions and documents regarding your income will be supplied by others, so watch your mail carefully. Mixed in with the usual junk are documents critical for your tax return. These include:

- a W-2 form from your employer, if you work for wages;
- a 1098 detailing how much interest you paid last year, if you own a home and have a mortgage;
- 1099 forms, if you are an independent contractor, own stock that paid dividends, or had interest or other types of non-wage income. If you have kept good records, you can match the 1099s against them. This double check not only helps catch any errors; it also keeps you from overlooking taxable income if the 1099 doesn't show up. If the IRS gets a copy of a 1099 and you don't, their computers will spot the underpayment and audit you for the money plus interest and possible penalties.

Now you are ready to begin entering the information on the tax forms, or to take the information to your accountant. (Many accountants will provide a worksheet for compiling information.)

## What Do You Need to Keep and for How Long?

Once you've finished filing your return, the next consideration is how long to keep the material you've collected. The simple answer is to keep whatever you need to persuade the IRS that everything on your return is accurate. Hang on to the evidence for as long as the IRS has the right to question your return.

Ordinarily, that's three years from the due date for the return, including extensions, to assess any additional tax. But a return can be audited for six years if the IRS suspects the taxpayer has neglected to report substantial income; if fraud is suspected, there is no time limit.

Your recordkeeping system doesn't have to be elaborate or sophisticated. What is more important is to have a system—and the discipline to keep the files up to date. Set up a separate reference file for each year's tax information, and separate it into folders for each itemized deduction: medical, taxes, interest, etc. Save any bills, receipts and canceled checks that correspond to those deductions. If you write off the cost of a business car, keep the logbook in which you recorded your trips as well as evidence of the costs you incur. Do you claim as a dependent someone who is not your child? If so, keep a separate file for the evidence that shows you provide more than half of that person's support.

You'll need to keep some records beyond the time the IRS requires for audit purposes. Homeowners need a file for the house to keep track of the cost of improvements they make while they own it (renovations, additions, etc.). These expenses will affect the profit when they sell the home. And investors must hang on to the documents that show what they paid and when they

| Action Notes |
| --- |

bought the investment. If you make nondeductible contributions to an individual retirement account and file tax form 8606, you need to keep the form and related information for your IRA sponsor until all funds have been withdrawn from the account. There are many other special circumstances, which should be discussed with a tax accountant.

When you clear out your tax files, err on the side of caution—particularly when it comes to your investments. As for the tax forms themselves, six years is probably long enough to hold on to them—except for those that have a bearing on future returns.

CHAPTER

FIFTEEN

# Your "To Read" Pile

**O**ne of the major challenges of paper management is the "To Read" pile. Most of us find it difficult to stay current with all of the newspapers, magazines and books we want to read. Add in the professional journals and newsletters, instruction guides for all those electronic gadgets we've got in the house, and promotional materials for insurance policies, self-improvement opportunities and candidates for political office. The task of keep-

*If your "To Read" pile is too high, you have three options: Read it, file it or throw it away.*

*Instead of taking time browsing through a magazine or journal, check the table of contents for articles that relate to your specific interest.*

ing up with our reading becomes overwhelming.

In many cases, the real issue of "To Read" is not to read, but to *remember*. The main reason to be "well-read" is that we want to be well-balanced in our knowledge so our lives will be more productive. We also feel we should read broadly because we worry we might miss something that could be very important to our lives, or at least be a lot of fun! And we'd like to be well-read to make a good impression on our friends and business colleagues.

There is a very positive aspect to an overflowing "To Read" pile. It shows that we have many interests, which is what makes us interesting, creative people. Remember that a creative mind always has more ideas than the body can carry out. Many of those ideas come from what we read, but what we must also remember is that there is no shortage of resources for ideas. There will always be more magazines and more newspapers. Spend your time reading, not feeling guilty over what you haven't read.

## Be Selective

The first step in solving the problem is to accept the fact that it is unlikely you will ever be able to read all the things you think you ought to read, let alone all the things you would like to read—even if you do take the best speed-reading course the country has to offer! The law of rising expectations will undoubtedly prevail: If you increase the speed at which you can read, the amount of information you want to read will also increase. So, although completing a speed-reading course may be a desirable goal, it will not solve the problem of the ever-growing "To Read" pile.

The issue is not reading faster, but reading smarter. One of the first rules is to be more selective. Instead of taking time browsing through a magazine or journal, check the table of contents for articles that relate to your specific interest. Read lead paragraphs, lead sentences and closing paragraphs to get the main idea. Beware of the lures of modern day marketing! Do you catch yourself reading a publication or major advertising promotion just because the promoter made it look so appealing, while at the same time ignoring a publication you must read to be current in your field?

Play a game with yourself to see how much potential reading material you can eliminate before it ever gets to your "To Read" pile. How much can go directly into the wastebasket, for example. Or, if you can't resist the temptation to read everything that comes into your house—even if you have no need to read it—take yourself off mailing and circulation lists. (See page 32 for the address you can write to do so.) Also, be particularly leery of those publications you receive as business perks. Ask yourself, "If I were paying for this publication out of my own pocket, would I still order?" If not, cancel it, or give it to someone who would benefit more from the subscription.

Make an inventory of the magazines and periodicals you receive each month. Estimate the amount of time it would take to read them the way you'd like to. Are your expectations realistic? If not, what can you do about it? Identify which publications contribute the most value. Consider alternating subscriptions every year or two.

*Play a game with yourself to see how much potential reading material can go directly into the wastebasket before it hits your "To Read" pile.*

## Improve Your Technique

When you have eliminated absolutely everything you think you can, try to improve your reading techniques.

One of the major stumbling blocks in reducing the "To Read" pile is perfectionism. For example, you receive an alumni newsletter in the mail. You are interested in the news of your former classmates, but there simply isn't time to read it now. So you put the newsletter on the credenza behind your desk or in the basket beside your lounge chair in the family room. And guess what? Six months later it's still there—along with the next five issues!

Or you receive a journal from your professional association. You feel obligated to keep up with the latest happenings and there are some activities in which you would like to participate, but there's no time to read the journal when it arrives. Into the basket it goes. By the time you get around to reading it a month later, the seminar that really suited your needs is filled or already over.

The end result in both of these cases is usually that you eventually tire of seeing the piles and toss everything out. No purpose is served in holding on to them except to create clutter and guarantee guilt!

There are no magic words to make your "To Read" pile disappear if it is too high. You have three options: Read it, file it or throw it away. If you choose the first option, you face a time-management problem. There is only one way to read, and that is to create the time to do it.

Make an appointment with yourself to read and mark it on your calendar, just as you would make an appointment with someone else to go to the movies. Consider your own biological rhythms. Is it easier to get up an hour earlier or stay up an hour later? Can you take your lunch to work two days a week and read through your lunch hour? To stay abreast with your business reading, can you set aside a "quiet time" each day, or two to three times a week, when your assistant will screen out all but the most important calls? Or can you put your phone on voice mail?

## *Incorporate*

Look for creative ways to incorporate reading into your daily life. Instead of driving to work, can you use public transportation or a car pool and use that time for reading? Do you travel frequently? If so, designate a place to put reading materials you can take with you on your next trip. Then use those inevitable delays as a gift of reading time instead of a total disaster.

Do you drive a car pool for your children and end up waiting for them, spend time waiting in doctor's offices or go to meetings that frequently begin late? Always carry reading materials with you so you can make the time productive.

I'm not suggesting that every uncommitted moment should be spent reading—or anything else. Sometimes the best way to use a few unexpected moments is to do some deep breathing or fantasize about a day at the beach! However, if you carry reading material with you, you can make a conscious choice instead of finding yourself in an unconscious trap. Keep in mind that it can be "fun reading!" One client of mine loves to read spy novels. He always carries one with him on airplanes—the only time he enjoys that relaxation luxury.

## Categorize Your Reading

**S**eparate your reading into types of reading. Keep all high priority reading together so that when you have set aside reading time you will not be tempted by material that belongs in a lower priority category.

Put material from other categories where it can be read as time permits. For example, many people enjoy reading mail-order catalogs when they want to relax. If you do, put a basket beside your bed where you can collect the catalogs, and read them at your leisure. But when the basket gets full, that's your signal it's time to toss some out—or start over completely.

Another category might be materials that you would like to read but that are not a high priority and will be outdated at a specific time. Jot down on the cover the deadline date for reading. If you haven't read it in, say, six weeks, or when the basket it full, throw the material out! This category of reading is a good one to carry with you when you're traveling. As you finish read-

### Tips for Effective Catalog Shopping

Write the name and page number of the items you're interested in on the front cover of the catalog. When you're ready to order, you'll be able to find the items quickly. Or tear out the pages, but be sure to jot down the phone number you'll need for ordering or tear out the mail order form—and throw the rest of the catalog away.

**Action Notes**

ing something, you can toss it out, offering the added incentive of lightening your luggage!

## Use Your Reference Files

Many people are hesitant to file away an article that they have not read because they're afraid it "may not be worth it." My experience has made it clear that we are more apt to read those articles that relate to the issues that are of particular importance at the moment. For example, if you find an article on planning a birthday party for a five-year-old and your son just turned four, your motivation to read the article will not be very great, but if his birthday is a month away you will be very interested in the information.

When you find an article that interests you but you don't have time to read it, tear out the article, file it according to the topic it relates to and discard the magazine. Then, when you are dealing with the topic, it will be much easier to determine if the article is useful. If the article remains in the pile of magazines behind your credenza, it's highly unlikely you'll remember the article, let alone have the time to go through the pile to find it!

If you frequently need to save articles related to your personal or professional interests, consider creating a separate file system that I call a "Library File." To determine where information should go, use the same question you ask for your reference files: "If I want to find this information, what word will I think of?" For example, an article about how to choose a caterer could go in a library file called "Entertaining," or an article on antique restorers could go in "Decorating" or "House Information."

A client of mine who is a physician scans the table of contents of his medical journals as they arrive, notes which articles he wants filed and jots in the margin the name of the file where the they should be filed. His assistant files the articles so they are available for his reading when he is dealing with a particular medical problem.

Always read with a pen in your hand. If you find a magazine article you'd like to save but can't tear it out because your spouse hasn't read the issue or there is another article of interest on the other side, just note the page number of the article (and the subject, if you wish) on the cover. Then, later on, when you're faced with stacks of old magazines, you will be able to identify quickly which contain articles you want to keep. (You may also discover some articles that interest you less than they did when you marked them!)

*Always read with a pen in your hand.*

## Set Limits

One of the most common questions from clients is "How long should I keep books, newspapers and magazines?" There is no right or wrong answer to this question. The answer depends entirely upon your feelings about these publications. For example, some people enjoy being around books, whether they have read them or not—or ever intend to read them. They appreciate books the way other people appreciate art or scenic views. If you feel that way about books and you have enough bookshelf space, by all means keep them.

However, if you're like me and too many books create stress, then eliminate those you've read and don't intend to read again and those either given to you (even if they did cost a fortune!) or that you picked up off the "Under $2.00" shelf in the local bookstore and that you never expect to read. But don't just throw them away! There are many more-productive uses for unwanted books, as discussed later in this chapter. As for the books you still want to read, make an appointment with yourself and get to it.

What about magazines and newspapers? Again, there is no right or wrong answer. Look at each publication individually and make a decision about how long you will keep it. For example, if you have young children, you may feel compelled to keep your *National Geographic* as reference material for future school projects. If

**Make an inventory of the magazines and periodicals you receive, then estimate how much time it would take to read them the way you'd like to do it.**

you really enjoy cooking or you entertain frequently, you may decide to keep *Gourmet* permanently. News magazines, however, are of little value when they are more than a week or two old, unless you happen to be a historian or a journalist.

I use the Sunday paper as my signal that it's time to discard the previous week's papers. If there are articles I really want to read but did not get around to it, I tear them from the paper and file them in my reference file as discussed earlier in this chapter. You may wish to photocopy newspaper articles. They can be reduced in size and therefore take up less file space. In addition, the photocopy will last longer than a newspaper copy.

Identify those items that are of extremely limited value when they become outdated. Last week's *TV Guide*, old phone books, catalogs from stores you've never ordered from, and last month's *Newsweek* are primary candidates for the trash!

If you really enjoy holding on to publications, what is the best way to do it? The first step is the same one we use in organizing so many things: "Put like objects together." For example, keep all travel books together, all kitchen magazines together, all catalogs together. If you like, put colored dots on book bindings to make it easy to keep them in the appropriate category. Put magazines in cardboard or plastic magazine holders—labeled with the name and year of publication. When you see the amount of one category you have accumulated, you can determine whether you really want to take up that much of your living space with that item.

If you do get rid of material, consider creating a card file, alphabetized by subject, so you can note a particular book, magazine or article that interested you. Then if it becomes important, you can easily retrieve the material from your local library. If you do not want a separate system, put the information in an existing file on that subject or inside another book you already have on the subject.

After you have categorized all your reading material and eliminated anything that you decide is excess, the final step is to designate a place to keep it. To determine that, ask yourself where you would be most likely to read or otherwise utilize the information. If it is reference material, in what room would you look for it? Travel and foreign language books might be best in the library or family room, while light fare such as *People* or *Reader's Digest* might go in a basket beside your lounge chair to read during commercials. Millions of us enjoy reading in the bathroom, so a magazine rack hanging on the back of the bathroom door might be the perfect place for the lightweight reading!

**Be particularly leery of those publications you receive as business perks.**

## Alternative Measures

If bookshelf space is a problem even after you have eliminated all the publications you can, then what? If you have some books that are important to the family but not particularly to you, identify your alternatives. Is there someone else in the family who would enjoy them more? If your children want them but are not in a position to take them now, put them in boxes in a safe, but less accessible location in your home— clearly labeled! If there is no available space, consider renting a self-storage unit.

If you have books that are no longer of interest to you or your family, donate them to a library or professional association, or sell them at a secondhand bookstore. If you have a large number of books, check your yellow pages to find a book dealer who will pick up the books at your house, so you can avoid the hassle of carting them around.

Consider alternatives to reading. There is nothing that says you are un-American if you don't read the daily newspaper (although you'll undoubtedly be a more informed one if you make a 15- to 30-minute appointment with yourself each day to read one). A friend of mine says it took him years to admit that he really could read all he wanted to of the newspaper by looking over the shoulder of the person standing next to him on the subway!

*In many cases, the real issue of "To Read" is not to read, but to remember.*

You can watch a half-hour nightly news broadcast at least a few times a week. There are also tapes that give summaries of news stories. Although at first you may think the cost is astronomical, consider the money you'll save on subscriptions and the time you'll save on read-ing—particularly if in the past you have been piling the newspapers up instead of reading them anyway!

Books on tape are a great way to relax or to educate yourself while commuting. I regularly listen to these tapes on my car's cassette player. In addition, I carry a small portable tape recorder so if I hear something that I want to act upon or make a note of I can record it. (I can also use the tape to make an oral note of something I think about as I'm driving.) When I reach my destina-tion, I transfer my recorded notes to my calendar, "To Do" list, rotary telephone file, reference files or other appropriate place. Taping parts of tapes is like saving articles of interest from a magazine instead of keep-ing the whole issue. In this instance, I avoid creating a tape pile.

A client of mine used to have all kinds of books, magazines and newspapers all over her house until she built a new house and discovered what it cost her per square foot. When she saw what her packrat behavior was costing her, she threw all the reading material out! Keep in mind that this country is full of libraries.

CHAPTER

SIXTEEN

# Your "To Write" Pile

If you want to see guilt written on the faces of a lot of people in a big hurry, just mention the word "letter writing!" The mobility of our society and our changing lifestyles have created an enormous network of people with whom we would like, or think we ought, to communicate. High divorce and remarriage rates result in larger, extended families. These and other changes in our lifestyles have complicated our lives and

*There will always be more people to write to than you have time for, so choose those who mean the most to you.*

*Write just one letter a week and you can communicate with 52 friends this year.*

made it even more difficult to keep up our written communication.

## Personal Correspondence

**A**s with every other aspect of paper management that we've discussed, the step in solving this paper problem is selectivity. There will always be more people to write to than you will have time for so choose those who mean the most to you. Keep in mind that circumstances change, and we do outgrow friendships. At twenty-five, you may have felt that your college roommate would always be an important relationship in your life, but now you realize that your paths led in different directions and there is little you have in common.

If you are serious about keeping up with your friends through letters, the most important thing to do is to set aside a regular time to write, such as one Sunday per month, or one letter before your favorite television program. And, remember, write just one letter a week and you can communicate with 52 friends each year.

Do whatever you can to make letter writing enjoyable and efficient. If that means using a computer or a typewriter, by all means do so! Some of us would never write to our family and friends if we had to write by hand—and in the case of a few people I know the recipients wouldn't be able to read the letters if we did! Personally, I love letters—all letters—and I have yet to criticize someone who wrote me on their PC.

If you're going to write, choose stationery and a pen that you like and find easy to use. Select different styles of writing paper for different occasions. Carry notepaper in your handbag or briefcase so you can jot a quick note while you wait for an appointment. This is also a great way to use postcards that you pick up while on vacation.

Thank you notes and letters of condolence are a major concern in the area of correspondence. Not only do we want to do what is socially correct, but we want people to know we appreciate their kindnesses and care about their suffering. In some cases you may find it's easier for you to make a telephone call than it is to write a letter. If you feel you must write a letter, do whatever you can to simplify the process. I find it helpful to purchase multiple copies of any thank you or sympathy cards I particularly like. If you don't have a card on hand and don't have time to get one, write a note on personal stationery.

We often put off writing a letter because there are so many things we want to say. But the longer we put it off, the more there is to write. Then we decide we will wait until Christmas, but the holidays come and go, and the Christmas cards that we did manage to purchase are still in the desk drawer. Finally, we are so embarrassed by our negligence that we completely lose contact with our friend.

If you recognize this scenario, ask yourself when was the last time you got a short note from a friend and complained, "My, that sure was a short note!" A short note is better than no note at all. Beware of perfectionism. Write what you can when you can, and the people who are truly friends will understand and be glad to hear from you.

## Birthdays and Anniversaries

There are a variety of ways to handle those annual special events. First, find a place to consistently list birthdays and anniversaries—a special occasion book, a section of your "To Do" book, or on a card in your rotary phone-file. (If you keep track of many dates, create one card for each month.)

Next you've got to find a way to remind yourself to look at the list. One person I know checks her list at the beginning of each month and transfers into her calendar the days she needs to mail the cards or gifts (not the day of the birthday, when it is frequently too late to take action). You may prefer to put all the reminders into your calendar at once for the entire year.

*Write what you can when you can and the people who are truly friends will understand and be glad to hear from you.*

One of the hazards of purchasing greeting cards that you see and like, even if you don't know to whom you will send them, is the risk of forgetting you have them—or not being able to find them at the right time. To avoid this situation, establish a specific place to keep the cards. Be sure that it is easily accessible if you want to encourage yourself to use them! If you keep more than 12 or 15 cards on hand, organizing them by occasion will save you time and prevent frustration. Use large envelopes (8 1/2″ × 11 1/2″), tuck in the flap to make a large pocket envelope, and write "Anniversary," "Birthday," etc. on the outside. Arrange the envelopes alphabetically, and put them in your reference file.

## Business vs. Pleasure

Again, it is very helpful to have stationery on hand that you can use for writing or typing business letters. You can often answer a business letter by writing a note on the letter itself (and keeping a copy for yourself only if necessary, rather than out of habit!). Another quick way to write a business letter is to use a postcard. I had some personalized ones printed to use for requesting information or confirming appointments.

Separate your "To Write" category into "Business" and "Personal." You may feel in the mood to write a quick thank you note but not to inquire about a discrepancy in your credit card bill. Sometimes you may find it convenient, or even fun, to take a box of note stationery and your "To Write—Personal" file with you to the doctor's office or the beach.

# CHAPTER

# SEVENTEEN

# Family Records

**A** Virginia father had to revaccinate his five-year old for school because he couldn't find the child's immunization card and the doctor who innoculated her was no longer in practice. A business executive missed an important financial opportunity when she needed to fly to Italy but couldn't find her passport. A financially struggling widow lost more than $2,000 in medical insurance reimbursements because she didn't file the claims within the two-year time limit.

What if you or your spouse—or both of you—suddenly died or became incapacitated? Would someone know where to find your will or what insurance benefits you have? What about the key to your safe deposit box? Could anyone find the cash stashed away in a money market fund? Suppose you need to make an overseas business trip or you want to sell some stock. Could you find your passport or records of the stock's purchase easily?

If any of these questions makes you feel uneasy, it is essential that you organize your records. As you do, you will be able to identify areas that need attention, such as out-of-date wills, inadequate homeowner's insurance, missing legal documents, or a beneficiary change you need to make on your insurance policy.

Chapter 11 explained how to organize and maintain

*It is essential that you organize your records. As you do, you will be able to identify areas that need attention.*

**121**

reference files. This chapter suggests what material should go into the folders.

## Bank Records

Your files should include the name and address of each bank, credit union, or savings and loan association where you have an account. Also include each type of account, the account numbers and signers of the accounts, as well as numbers of CDs and the location of passbooks, statements and CDs.

Many banks block joint accounts when they receive notification of death of one of the joint owners. If this is the case, each spouse may wish to set up a separate emergency account in his or her own name. Ask your bank to write you a letter stating its policy, so you know beforehand.

## Credit Cards and Charge Accounts

List account numbers and names of issuers so that lost or stolen cards can be promptly reported missing. In the event of death, survivors can notify issuers of the cards and inform banks if accounts are to be closed or listed in a different name.

## Tax Records

Be sure that family members know where to locate information for filing income tax returns and where you keep records from previous years. Chapter 14 has detailed information on this subject.

## Investment Records

While the monetary rewards resulting from investments can create a great sense of security, for many people the paper generated by those investments often creates a great sense of insecurity! One of my clients had a four-drawer filing cabinet filled with annual reports dating back more than a decade. She had never read any of them, but she was convinced she should keep them—just in case!

Investment companies send many different kinds of

information. Some can be thrown out immediately; some needs to be kept until you've made a decision on the information; some material needs to be kept as long as you keep a particular security. For example, investment companies regularly send material intended to inform you of their recommendations for stock purchases. If you decide not to buy the stock, you don't need to keep their recommendation. But if you do act on the information, you'll need to keep the subsequent records of the purchase, along with statements that show how much the investment appreciates or depreciates so you'll have an accurate record when you eventually sell the stock and have to figure your tax on the transaction.

Keep a separate file for essential information, including your monthly statements and the confirmations of your various transactions, as opposed to the generic information that is sent to all investors. Here's an outline of the kind of information you should have in your files:

### Stocks, bonds and mutual funds

Where are the certificates kept? List name and address of brokers, list of holdings, including owner's name, date bought and purchase price for each security.

### Keogh, IRA, 401(k) plans

For each family member, include name of institution and location of papers.

### Other investments

For *collectibles,* what kind do you have? Where are they kept? Who should appraise them for sale or insurance purposes?

If you own *businesses,* what type are they? Where are they located? Where do you keep important documents relating to them (in a safe at the business, or your safe deposit box, for example). Who should be contacted if there's a problem?

If you own *real estate,* note who else owns the property if it is held jointly. This includes property owned jointly by married persons. If the joint owner is

| Action Notes |
| --- |
|  |

not a spouse, give the name, address, and interest of each joint owner.

Include the name and address of the mortgagee, how the property is titled, the date of acquisition and cost, mortgage terms including the original amount, the monthly payment and the payment due date, and date of final payment.

### Retirement Income Records

In planning ahead for retirement, it is extremely important for you and your spouse to have a complete up-to-date record of your pension plan or plans, any annuities you will receive, rents or royalties and your estimated social security benefits. You can obtain a leaflet "Estimating Your Social Security Check" from your nearest social security office, and you can obtain a statement of your social security earnings by sending a "Request for Statement of Earnings" form to the Social Security Administration. These forms are available from your local office.

In most families, one person handles most financial matters. If you've been the family controller, you know the intricacies of the situation. Continuity in planning and implementing financial strategies is important, and while you can't expect someone else to follow your exact track, you want your successor to understand what you have been doing. This means that in addition to listing where the assets are you should provide information on managing any complicated situations to help your successor take charge of your affairs.

### Trusts

List any trusts you have created or trusts created by others under which you possess any power, beneficial interest or trusteeship. Include the name of the trust, location, trustee and beneficiary.

### Wills

For couples, the importance of both parties having up-to-date wills cannot be overemphasized. The individual who makes no will forfeits any assurance that his or her property will be distributed according to his or her wishes, and will probably cause unnecessary difficulties and possible financial losses for the survivors. When a person dies without a will, the distribution of the estate is governed by state laws that may not fit the best interest of the family.

Review your will periodically. If you have married, divorced or remarried, if heirs have been born or died, if the size or nature of your estate has changed, or if you have moved to a different state, your will needs to be updated.

*If you die without a will, you forfeit any assurance that your property will be distributed according to your wishes.*

## Liabilities Records

There are two primary reasons for keeping a complete liabilities record. First, should you become ill and require hospitalization, your family should know not only to whom you owe money, but also when payments are due to avoid unnecessary complications. Second, should you die, a comprehensive record of your liabilities serves as a basis to dismiss any false claims made against your estate.

Include installment debts on home(s), automobile, credit cards, home improvements, personal loans, furniture, appliances and business loans. Information needed includes current balances, monthly payments, due dates, and whether there is debt insurance.

## Insurance Records

The information about your policies are important for two reasons. In the event of your death, it ensures that your family and executor of your estate will know what insurance benefits are available, which companies and insurance agents to contact and how to file claims. In addition, should you become incapacitated due to accident or illness your family will be able to pay policy premiums to keep your coverage in force.

Automobile and homeowners insurance policies should be kept in your reference files so you can refer to them quickly to update or check coverage.

Life insurance policies should be in your safe deposit box, but keep information in your files identifying the name of the company for each policy, the policy number, face amount, beneficiaries, whether there has been a loan taken on the policy, premium due date, and the name of the agent.

Also keep medical insurance policies in your files because you will need to refer to them when making claims. The simplest, most effective way to keep track of the status of insurance claims is to create three file folders. Every insurance claim falls into one of these stages, so it's simple to check on the status of any claim at any time as it moves through the system.

Label the first "Medical Insurance—To Be Submitted." This contains the blank claim forms, the instructions on how to submit a claim and any receipts from the doctor, laboratory, clinic or pharmacy. Label the second file folder "Medical Insurance—Submitted, But Not Paid." This contains a photocopy of the patient copy of any claims you submitted for reimbursement but for which you have not yet received payment. Finally, the third folder is labeled, "Medical Claims—Paid." This information should be kept for three years to support any medical deduction taken on your tax return.

### Medical Records

In addition to insurance records, it is important to keep individual medical records. The simplest method is to establish a separate file for each family member ('Medical—Mary" and "Medical—John," for example). Include doctor and dental receipts that identify diseases and treatments. (These can be culled from the "Health Insurance—Paid" file). Also note in these files information about blood type, eyeglass prescriptions, and allergies.

Finally, many people like to keep articles about medical *developments* or pamphlets they pick up at the doctor's office or the pharmacy. Do not include this information in your medical records file. Make a separate file for these informational materials, for example, "Medical Information—Coronary Care."

## Survivor's Benefits Records

Tragically, many survivor's benefits are left unclaimed because the survivors are unaware of their availability. These benefits are not paid automatically. Applications must be made on prescribed forms and specific documents furnished.

The most well known benefit is social security. Survivors of deceased veterans or active-duty service personnel are also eligible for benefits through the Veterans Administration. These benefits do not conflict with claims made under social security, but again, they are not paid automatically. In most cases, claims must be made within two years following death.

There are several other possible sources of survivor's benefits, including Worker's Compensation, employer's insurance policy, life insurance policy, health/accident policy, auto/casualty insurance, trade union, and fraternal organizations.

Keep all relevant policies, addresses, phone numbers and persons to contact in your files, and be sure your family is aware of these benefits and where the information is filed.

## In Case of Ill or Aging Family Members

Admittedly, this is one of the most difficult areas of paper management, but it is also one of the most important. Make sure your own records are in order and that someone knows where you keep them. In addition, be sure you or another family member possesses or has access to the information for any family members for whom you or they are responsible.

You will need a Power of Attorney if that person dies or becomes unable to make his or her own decisions. In addition to dealing with matters necessary in the event of death (as outlined on the following page), changes in records also need to be made for automobile titles, stocks and bonds, bank accounts, etc.

Here's one more very important thing to consider: Be sure to include any special instructions to the family about your memorial service, funeral, or burial preferences. It will be a big comfort to your family. A friend of mine said she felt so badly when her mother died because she did not know whether she wanted her wedding ring left on when she was buried.

## In Case of Death . . .

You may not like to think about such things, but by planning ahead, some of the stress involved when a family member dies can be eliminated. Here are some lists of information someone in the family should have, or have access to.

| To get a burial permit, you will need: | You will need these documents: | You will need to notify: |
|---|---|---|
| Name, home address, telephone number | Deeds to property, automobile title(s) | Doctor or health maintenance organization |
| How long in state | Insurance policies | Funeral director or memorial society |
| Occupation and title | Income tax returns | Institution to which remains may be donated if living will exists. |
| Name address and phone number of business | Military discharge papers | |
| Social security number | Disability claims | Memorial park |
| Armed Service serial number | Birth Certificate or other legal proof of age | Relatives, friends, employers of deceased |
| Date and place of birth | Citizenship papers, if naturalized | Insurance agents |
| Citizenship | Will | Attorney, accountant or executor of estate |
| Father's name and birthplace | Social security card | Religious, fraternal, civic, veteran's groups |
| Mother's maiden name and birthplace | Death certificate (certificates for burial permit) | Newspapers regarding death notices |
| | Bank books | |
| | Marriage and divorce certificates, if any | |

## Family History Records

The purpose of this category is to assemble in one place important family information that might be necessary to obtain a passport, apply for social security and veterans benefits or to file a loan application. For each family member include birth date (copy of birth certificate if available; original should be in safe deposit box), social security number, and copy of marriage or divorce certificate. Any family genealogy records can also be kept here.

Include in this file the names and phone numbers for your accountant, financial planner, employee-benefits advisor, insurance agents (life, health, car, personal property, homeowners), stockbroker, or other financial advisor.

## Education, Employment and Military Records

Keep a separate file for each family member. For example, "Education Records—Paul" and "Military Records—Bob." The information in these files simplify the task of writing or rewriting a resume, applying for admission to an educational institution, or applying for a new job. Besides, who knows—someone may want to write your biography one day.

## Household Inventory

One of the most neglected family records is the household inventory. If there is a fire or burglary in your home, this record will help you remember what has to be replaced and determine the value of each item. An inventory is also an excellent way to make certain that your insurance protection is sufficient. One client of mine purchased a $15,000 painting but neglected to add it to his insurance policy. When someone accidentally damaged the painting, the owner had to pay for repairs himself.

When you make an inventory, start at one point in the room and go all the way around, listing everything. The more complete the information, the more valuable it will be. Include information such as initial cost, model

**When you** **your hou** **photos o** **and special items** **so that identifying** **or replacing them** **will be easier.**

numbers, brand names and descriptions. Take photographs of the room and special items so that identifying or replacing them will be easier. Videotapes make excellent inventories. Be sure to include the basement, garage and attic. Estimate the replacement cost for each item and add up the total to determine how much insurance you should have. As you take inventory, mark your property with some identification. Your police department may have a special identification program. You can also purchase engravers to mark items with a code you think up.

Update your inventory every six months or so by adding recent purchases and adjusting replacement costs. Some insurance policies automatically increase replacement costs. Be sure you know the limits in your homeowner's policy with regard to valuables such as jewelry, furs, and art.

If you find the task of preparing a household inventory overwhelming, check your yellow pages and find a professional to do it, or get other members of the family to help you. Keep the records in a fireproof safe at home or your safe deposit box.

### *Warranties and Instructions*

One of the major joys or major frustrations of the American kitchen in the 20th Century is the kitchen gadget. It is a joy when you can find it when you need it, but it's a major frustration when you can't remember how to operate it—and you can't find the instruction book!

Every time you purchase a new appliance, toy, tool, or other household item, you are blessed with several new pieces of paper: a consumer registration card; a promotion brochure for other products manufactured by the same company; an instruction booklet; and, frequently, a consumer questionnaire. To further complicate matters, often a company will issue the same warranty for several products. Just because you can find a warranty doesn't mean you will know what it protects!

To minimize this problem, there are several steps you can take.

**1. Decide where you will keep all warranty and instructional information.**

I do not recommend separating them because often one piece of paper will have the warranty and the instruction. You may decide to keep those related to kitchen appliances in the kitchen so they will be readily available, or if your kitchen storage space is limited, you may choose to put them in the household reference file under "Warranties and Instructions." Frequently it is helpful to put the instruction booklet with the stereo, telephone or tape recorder so you can refer to it easily. Keep instructions relating to clothing in a plastic bag in the laundry room.

**2. Keep the receipt with the warranty.**

Whenever you make a purchase, staple the receipt to the warranty information so you can easily prove date of purchase, or put the date on the front of the warranty for your own information.

**3. Decide now whether you will or will not fill out consumer information cards and warranty registration cards.**

We often take longer shuffling the card than it would take to fill it out! Usually, the manufacturer doesn't require that you complete the cards to make the warranty valid, but it is helpful to manufacturers and is essential if you need to be reached for product recall.

## *Safe Deposit Box*

Keep papers that are difficult or impossible to replace in a safe deposit box. The box should be large enough to hold everything that should be in it—and small enough to keep out things that do not need to be there. The box should not be used as a catchall for souvenirs.

Keep in your reference file at home a list of everything you have in your safe deposit box. Update the list as you add or remove items. If you store documents from investment properties or securities, the rental can be claimed as a deduction on your tax return.

Finally, make sure family members know where the box is located and where the key is kept.

---

### What to Keep in Your Safe Deposit Box

Adoption papers
Automobile titles
Birth certificates
Citizenship papers
Copies of wills (original, in most cases, should be kept with County Registrar of Wills)
Death certificates
Divorce decrees
Government or court recorded documents
Household inventory and negatives from pictures (include appraisals and receipts)
Important contracts
Leases
Life insurance policies
List of insurance policy names and numbers
Marriage certificate
Military records
Passports
Patents and copyrights
Property deed and other mortgage papers
Retirement plans
Stock and bond certificates and notes

# Family Memorabilia and Photographs

*A picture may be worth a thousand words, but an unidentified picture is worth little to future generations.*

It's September. The summer vacations, family gatherings and neighborhood barbecues were great fun. But all that remain are warm memories, 37 envelopes of photographs and 13 videotapes that pop up like mushrooms all over the house but are nowhere to be found when you want to show them to someone! Add to that the boxes of old, unidentified family photographs your mother passed on to you for safekeeping, the trunk of

family memorabilia you married along with your husband, and the piles of creative clutter your children produce. There seems to be no relief in sight.

## Feelings, Feelings

One of the major problems with photographs and other memorabilia is all the emotion involved. Even if we have no interest in them ourselves, we feel that we should have some interest because they represent our family history. How do you know what your heritage will be while you are living it? We feel burdened because the memorabilia was so important to our parents or because it might be important to our yet unborn grandchildren. In the meantime, what do we do with all the stuff? It fills our attics and basements with boxes and our minds with guilt.

If you are facing that dilemma, there are several steps you can take. First, recognize that is there no right or wrong approach. To decide what you want to do, begin gathering information about the alternatives you may have. Determine who else might be involved in the decision-making process.

It's not possible to foresee exactly how your descendants will feel about this information. You can only make your decisions based on your current conditions and resources.

## It Only Seems Hopeless

When you consider the amount of love, time and money that have gone into your memorabilia thus far you feel obligated to do something. The question is, "What?"

The simple baby books and photo albums like those our mothers used are no longer adequate for most families. Your intentions are good, but the mechanics of the task seem overwhelming—and even if you have the motivation, where do you find the time? How do you begin? What if you don't have the motivation? Can you risk ignoring the issue? And what about the space all this memorabilia takes in your house that you could be using for something else?

The most important step in dealing with the situation is to recognize that if left unchecked it is only going to get worse. As life goes on, the memorabilia continues to accumulate. If the old stuff is out of control just think what another year's worth will be like!

Instead of wasting energy berating yourself every time you open the closet door and see those boxes of photographs, decide what action you can take to stop the cycle, and then do it. As with so many other aspects of paper management, the way to begin to make progress on this seemingly impossible task is to start with material you collect from today on. For the time being, ignore those piles of yesterday's memories. You can work on the backlog after you have devised a system that works for you.

## One Woman's Sensible Solution

**O**ne of my clients had a particularly difficult time dealing with her photographs. Keeping up with them was a continual frustration. She decided to come up with a system to correct it—one that fit her needs and circumstances—and that is exactly what she did.

She began by deciding not to bring photographs home until she had taken certain steps at her office. First, she throws away any photographs that she does not like for whatever reason.

Next, she dates the photos and makes any necessary notations on them. She doesn't allow this step to become overwhelming, causing her to procrastinate about the project altogether! She has made a commitment to herself that the date is the only absolute requirement. (I would add to that names so years from now you'll know who's in the picture.)

Then she prepares a pile of heavy envelopes addressed to her parents and her in-laws. Her photo-processing store charges very little for duplicate prints, so she orders them automatically and sends selected duplicates to the relatives. (If you do not order duplicates but have some photos you want to duplicate, designate an envelope for those negatives that you need to return to the store for duplicating.) Whatever duplicates she does not send to her family and friends she throws away immediately. This step not only minimizes the number of photographs she has to deal with at home, but it pleases the grandparents immensely.

Finally, she puts the remaining photographs into the plastic pages the photo-processing store gives her when she pays for the pictures. All she has to do when she gets home is put the pages in a looseleaf notebook.

One of the extra bonuses resulting from her solution is that other members of her family have become much more interested in the photos because they are easily visible instead of buried in boxes in the closet!

She has since applied similar systems to other paper problems with success. She didn't think she had the discipline to do it, but she did. And you can too.

## Make It Easy on Yourself

As with other aspects of paper management, you've got to recognize that you probably won't have the time to organize family memorabilia as perfectly as you'd like. Determine what you're willing and able to do, and do it.

As my client did with her photographs, design a system to fit *your* particular needs. Start by identifying an accessible place where you will put all the memorabilia as you receive it or find it.

If you have a small amount, two boxes labeled "Photographs" and "Memorabilia" (napkins, brochures, invitations, matchbooks, dried flowers, etc.) may be all you'll need. If you have difficulty putting things away in their proper place, leave the lids off the boxes so

*The more information you know, the more joy the photo will bring in the years to come—who, what, where, when, why.*

they will be easier for you to use. At the end of the year, put the lids on the boxes, clearly label them (for example, "Photos—1987") and put them away. If you are short on storage space, put your boxes in an out-of-the-way location, such as the attic or basement. (Be careful not to store the boxes near a heat source or where it's moist. You don't want to go to the time and trouble of storing valued memories only to find them ruined.) Then note where they are on your reference-file index (See Chapter 11).

Take whatever steps you can to make the organization process *easier*. If you don't have time to go through and label each picture, make a note on the outside of the photo envelope as to the major categories, "Summer—1965," or "Jerry's Birthday Party—1987," for example. You might also have your photos developed at a lab that dates the back of your photos. (Remember, the date indicates when the film is developed, not when you took the pictures.) You can buy a camera attachment that dates the photo when you take it!. Put a date on memorabilia such as travel brochures, napkins, etc. as you receive it.

You will be able to re-create the occasion more easily if you decide to organize the materials in a more sophisticated style.

If you are a "memoraholic," you may need to divide your treasures into smaller categories to make them more manageable. There are several ways you can do that. For example, if you have more than one child you may wish to have a photo album or memorabilia box for each one. Or you may want to create categories by type such as "Children's Art," "Playbills," "Trips." These can be further broken down by destination and date, such as "Europe—1990."

## Kids Can Get Involved, Too

If you have children who are old enough to be involved in the decision-making, ask them how they feel about the issue. You can give family memorabilia to your children, but be sure to do so with "no strings attached." Let them decide what to do with it based on their own needs and perspectives. If you feel strongly about what should happen to a particular keepsake and would be hurt if your children didn't follow your wishes, keep it yourself—or find someone who agrees with your wishes.

Perhaps you've got material that's not important to you or your children. Ask a professional buyer of memorabilia if what you've got has any particular value to other people. If it does, perhaps you can give it to a charity, or sell it to a collector.

If you or your children feel it is important to go through everything yourselves to determine what you should keep, you'll need to develop a system for doing that. When time is a major factor, you may find it necessary or desirable to hire a professional organizing consultant to help you. If your children think it should be done, get a commitment from them as to how and when they will help.

## *Doing It Alone*

If you are going to sort through your memorabilia alone, make a plan for accomplishing the task. Will you have to do it in bits and pieces or is it possible to spend several days working on the project? In either event, set goals for yourself. When you are having guests for dinner after work you can fix dinner in an hour if you need to, but if you have all day Saturday you can spend hours preparing dinner. This project works the same way. The more time you allow, the more it will take.

If you have a home with plenty of storage space your decisions about what to keep may be different from someone who lives in a small apartment. Off-site storage is a possibility if you have no space in your home. Be sure to compare prices when choosing one, and decide whether it is important to store the belongings close by or whether you can use a storage facility some distance away, which may save you money.

*The first candidates for the wastebasket are double exposures and those fascinating shots of the inside of your lens cap.*

If you're having trouble parting with some items but don't have enough space, consider ways of using memorabilia in your home or office. Thanks to the help of a creative friend, I now enjoy decorating with many memorabilia treasures that used to be buried in drawers, taking up room and never seen or enjoyed.

## Memorabilia Scrapbooks

Memorabilia scrapbooks for special mementos other than photographs require a great deal of patience and creativity because many of them come in odd shapes and sizes. If you enjoy such projects you can have a ball, but if you don't it's probably unrealistic to expect much success at doing it. I recommend just leaving the items in your "Memorabilia" box.

## The Knack of Good Photo-Albuming

If you have taken all, or even some, of the steps described thus far, don't be surprised if one day you discover you really are ready to get those photographs into albums. It's a terrific project when you are housebound for one reason or another. Take whatever steps you can to get into the right frame of mind. Look on the process as a wonderful adventure into memory land. Get into comfortable clothes, put on your favorite music, fix a pot of coffee (but don't put it where you risk ruining any photographs if it spills!), and you're on your way! Take the following steps:

**1. Choose a good place to work.**
Work in a comfortable chair at a large, clean, flat surface in an area where there's plenty of light and where you can leave the project until it is completed—or at least long enough to make some major progress. Resist the urge to rush out and buy photo albums at this point!

138

Time will give you a better idea of the kind and quantity you need.

## 2. Sort through the photos.

Eliminate all those unsuccessful shots. Don't be discouraged—even professional photographers use only a small percentage of the photos they take. The first candidates for the wastebasket are double exposures and those fascinating shots of the inside of your lens cap! Very close behind are pictures you wish had been double exposures—like the one that shows only the lower half of your body—and those shots you wonder why you took (the one of the Christmas tree after you took down the decorations).

## 3. Give away photos you won't use.

Many photos have little meaning to you, but could be special to someone else. They are fun to drop in the mail, and you will undoubtedly bring a quick smile to Aunt Amanda's face!

## 4. Identify the negatives.

Before you separate the pictures from their negatives, write a description on the outside of the packet, such as "Graduation—John, 1991," or simply use dates, and put the negatives in the packet. You may decide that once you have the picture and as many copies as you want you can throw the negatives away. If you want an "insurance policy" against unexpected disasters such as theft, fire or other loss (or divorce), keep the negatives in a separate place. Perhaps you could exchange negatives with a family member—or put negatives of favorite shots in your safe deposit box.

## 5. Identify the photos.

Determine whether you are going to put the information about the photo on the back of the photo or on a separate piece of paper so that it could be read after the photos are in albums. (Some energetic people do both!). The more information you know, the more joy the photo will bring in the years to come—who, what, where, when, and why. Experience has proven that, while a picture may be worth a thousand words, an unidentified picture is worth little to future generations.

### 6. Categorize the photos.

Sort photos into the categories you plan to use in the albums. Most people sort chronologically, but some do it by subject matter—for example, "Family Reunions." CAUTION: Label the piles as you work. If you are interrupted it won't take long to proceed with the sorting. One easy way to do this is to purchase inexpensive small baskets that can be labeled temporarily with removable labels.

### 7. Select albums.

Now is the time to decide what kind of albums you wish to use. A loose-leaf photograph album has a distinct advantage if you are trying to arrange photos chronologically because it's easy to add a page if you find more photos after you finish the project.

If you want to limit the number of albums you'll need, you may prefer the kind in which the photos are in individual sleeves, overlapping one another. The disadvantage of this type is that it will not accommodate oversized photos.

### 8. Into the album they go.

Let your creativity loose! Enjoy experimenting with different arrangements. Feel free to trim photos to their best advantage. If you have several photos from one event, group them together on one or more pages and write a short scenario about the occasion, rather than labeling each photo individually.

## Slides, Films and Tapes

Slides to organize? Label in pen directly on the cardboard frame. Write so that you can look at the slide with the naked eye and read the label at the same time. This will be a big advantage should you ever want to put together a slide show.

Movies and videotapes should be organized, too. The key is to label them clearly. Keep peel-off labels and a felt-tipped pen in the same drawer or shelf as you keep your photographic equipment. Label as you go—even if you don't have time to do it perfectly.

## Be Creative

**A**s you browse through your photos, consider ways of using your favorites in some unusual way. Check with your local photographic-supply or film-processing shop for ideas. Here are some possibilities:

**Make your own picture postcards.**
"Photo Talk" stickers are available from a photographic supply store. You can use the stickers to add amusing comments above people's heads.

**Make a photo T-shirt.**
Take a color print that is the size you want to a copy shop that has a heat-transfer machine. Have a transfer made and applied to a T-shirt, or take the transfer home and apply it yourself, as you would an iron-on patch.

**Make a jigsaw puzzle.**
Companies advertise this service in the classified section of magazines, or check your local photo-finishing store. A great gift idea!

**Make a poster.**
Turn your pictures into artwork to hang in your family room or college dorm room. Consider panoramic views of places that are special to you. The same companies that make jigsaw puzzles can do this for you.

*Many photos have little meaning to you, but could be special to someone else. They are fun to drop in the mail, and you will undoubtedly bring a quick smile to Aunt Amanda's face!*

**Make a calendar.**

Custom photo-finishing labs are equipped to print a photo above a twelve-month calendar. This makes a great holiday gift idea for children, grandparents, friends or business associates.

**Make a videotape from a slides or photos.**

Some photography stores will do this, or your video store may be able to refer you to an individual who specializes in custom-made videotapes from slides and prints.

The next time a grandparent or other elderly family member is celebrating a birthday or other special occasion and you cannot think of a suitable present, ask if they have any old photographs. Chances are they will, and nothing would please them more than to have your help in putting them in albums.

My grandmother talked for years about all the photographs she had never labeled. She was concerned that she couldn't remember everything about the pictures and that her handwriting was not good enough for future generations. I invited her to tell me about the photos while I made notes. Eventually I found at least one picture of every member in both grandparent's families. Whenever anyone comes to visit, it takes her only a few minutes to find the photo album. And the reminiscing begins. It's still not clear who received the greatest gift.

## *Keep Those Cards and Letters Coming*

What do you do about all those beautiful greeting cards you have received for birthdays, anniversaries and other special events? What about all the letters from relatives and friends? If you keep them, you may feel guilty because they take up so much room, and if you toss them you may feel guilty because you care about the people who sent them or you think they're too pretty to throw away.

There is nothing wrong with keeping every card and

letter you ever received if you have plenty of space to store them and you enjoy looking at them—or just entertain the possibility that you might someday! If, however, you feel a knot in your stomach every time you see them or you don't have a place to put the stationery you need for answering today's mail, then you would be wise to reconsider your actions.

One viable solution for letters is to select the ones that contain information that would be of particular interest in the future. I enjoy saving the letters from my mother that describe special family events, for example.

The method you use for keeping cards and letters will be determined by the way you plan to use them. If you are keeping them strictly for casual reading in the years to come, a box labeled "Letters to Save" will do nicely. If, however, you want to be able to refer to them you should keep them accessible. Try filing them alphabetically in an accordion-type file with alphabet dividers.

I put all the cards I receive for a particular occasion on the mantle in the family room. After two or three weeks, I keep only those that are particularly special— and in some cases I throw them all away because I know there are others, and I am optimistic enough to believe there will be more! A friend of mine keeps all of hers and then every few years makes a collage of them to hang as a decoration. Another frames cards she finds particularly beautiful. Some community groups collect them to use in self-help projects for handicapped persons and senior citizens. Sometimes schools are happy to have them for art projects. (See "Recycling" in Chapter 6.)

Whatever you decide to do with them, remember that the sender intended that card or letter to bring joy, not stress—so enjoy!

*Enjoy experimenting with different arrangements. Feel free to trim photos to their best advantage.*

# NINETEEN

# The Kitchen Papers

The kitchen or eating area is the "heart" of many if not most homes. It's easy to see how it can also become a catchall for a multitude of paper—the newspaper that you left on the table when you hurried off to work or a morning school carpool; the school papers your kids brought home and dumped on the counter; the mail you grabbed out of the mailbox as you raced in the door (now sorted in several unidentified piles!); and the notes, phone

messages and recipes that are piled on any available surface. What can you do to sort all this out?

## Kitchen Catch-All

The first step is to create a gathering place to put all
the paper when you don't have time to put it away. You
could use a large basket, a shelf or a tray. The key to
success in kitchen-paper management is to make an appointment with yourself to get back to the pile before it
becomes too overwhelming, to separate what should
come out of the catch-all from what really belongs in the
kitchen. You may find it helpful to do it on a regular
basis—before your favorite television show, or once a
month when you pay bills.

Keep the catch-all pile as small as possible by putting things away whenever you can. For example, if as
you pick up the mail you see several pieces of "junk
mail," throw them away immediately. It will also be
much easier to keep the papers in the kitchen at a mini-
mum if you have specific places for papers to go—unread
newspapers under the coffee table in the family room;
read newspapers on the floor in the front hall closet or in
the garage to be saved for a scout drive or community
recycling program, or thrown out.

If your work center is in the kitchen, put the papers
you need to act on in your "To Sort" tray until you are
ready to take action on them. If your work center is in
another room, take your paper there whether it is an
office, your family room, bedroom or basement. Put the
papers that belong to other family members in places
designated for their attention.

## Message Mania

One of the annoying results of our telephone-laden
world is a myriad of notes—some written to us by others
who have taken our telephone messages, some written by

## Put It on the Fridge

Communication can be a constant frustration in families, particularly in homes where there is a single parent or where both parents are working. To improve the situation, designate a communication center that is convenient for everyone. The refrigerator is usually a good place. It's also the place to put chore reminders. But be sure your messages aren't always things to do. You can also communicate nonessential, but very important messages, such as "Hope you had a good day at school. I love you. Mom."

us to ourselves as we talk or plan to talk on the phone.

What can you do to avoid, or at least minimize, this problem? How many times a week do you find a piece of paper with notes from several different telephone conversations? The major question is, "Where do I put it?" One very simple solution is to get a small notepad by the phone—I like 5" x 7"—and use one piece of paper, more if necessary, for each call. When the conversation is over, ask yourself, "What is the next action required on this piece of paper?" The answer will tell you where to put it. (For more details on this process, see Chapter 10.) In many instances, all you need to do is double check to see that the number is in your telephone-number system, then you can throw away one more piece of paper.

Be sure to designate a place where family members can check to see if they have phone messages. You can use a bulletin board, a plastic message holder, magnets on the refrigerator or envelopes attached to the wall or a door. Be sure the owner's names are clearly labeled so there is no confusion! Encourage family members to note on the message the date and time they took the call.

One of the major factors in organizing the papers related to your phone is actually returning calls. All the organization in the world will not make the papers go away. Only you, or someone to whom you delegate, can do that. See pages 54 and 55 for some time-management tips that can help with regard to phone calls.

To keep your message center organized, find one place to put all the papers that require calls. Put them in a file folder with a label "Call," or in a pile near your phone. Or make a list of the people you need to call and throw out the individual notes. To save time, also note the phone numbers on the list. Then when you have time to make one phone call it won't require much more time to make two or three.

And consider getting an answering machine. (Or see if you phone company offers an answering service.) Whether you like them or not, answering machines are a fact in our society, so it is in your best interest to accept them and to learn to use them to your advantage. When you do, you will never again have to accept "I tried to call you, but you were never home!"

You'll discover the machines can do many things. I have one that answers two phone lines with separate messages. I can determine which line will be answered by machine and can change the message when I'm away. I call home and, by pushing one number, the machine will tell me how many calls I have received. Then it plays each of the messages and tells me which line the call came in on, and at what time. At the end of the message, the machine tells me what to do if I want to erase the messages, save the messages, or change my message.

The machine also has a "memo" capability so that if my children want to give me a message but do not know where I am, or don't feel like writing it down, they can talk into the machine and it will record their message!

That machine has simplified my life more than any kitchen appliance I ever purchased. (My heart nearly stopped one day when I checked my messages and the machine announced, "I detect a malfunction. Please check your message!" Amazing!).

*Answering machines are a fact of life in our society. Accept them and learn to use them to your advantage.*

## Kitchen Transitions

**O**bviously some papers belong in the kitchen— recipes, cookbooks, entertainment records, coupons (if you are a user not just a collector), and take-out menus.

Your attitude toward the kitchen, and toward cooking, will determine to a great extent how your kitchen should be organized. There are many factors that contribute to our feelings, and it is also important to acknowledge that these feelings change with time and circumstances. This does not mean we are being lazy or negligent, just that our priorities have changed.

Frequently I find clients who are overwhelmed with guilt from the piles of papers in the kitchen because they are afraid to admit that they are not as interested in cooking as they once were. If fact, I'm a good example. When I was first married, my husband and I entertained often. We had three children and we were on a limited budget. For all of these reasons, I spent a considerable amount of time with papers in the kitchen—collecting coupons, selecting recipes, keeping records of what I served guests, educating myself about the nutritional needs of my children, and reading the food columns in the newspapers.

Later, I was divorced and my children were with me only part time. I ate out often and devoted the energy previously spent in the kitchen on my career. Then I married a man who has two children.

With five teenagers in and out of our home, the organization needs in the kitchen have changed drastically. Because family members—and their friends—are in and out frequently, it's important to have lots of food possibilities at a moment's notice.

I am once again interested in recipes, but very different ones from those that interested me 15 years ago. For example, I used to believe that if I didn't spend at least an hour preparing the evening meal, no compliment was justified. Now I look for 10-minute recipes that generate smiles—or at least fill stomachs! In addition, most of my cooking now is done in the microwave. And I'm much more conscious of the nutritional value of what we eat. Entertaining is much more informal, so souffles that have to be eaten the moment they come out of the oven are of little interest. Dishes that can be prepared in advance of the event are essential.

Once I understood that my circumstances had changed, I went through all my old recipes, and the recipes I intended to try. If a recipe didn't fit my time requirements or the dish would not be healthy, I threw the recipe out—at least most of them!

## *Designing Your Cookbook and Recipe System*

Let's take a look at the issue of recipes and cookbooks. First of all, accept the fact that you may not organize your recipes and cookbooks the same way your mother did. That does not mean you are wrong—just different, because your lifestyle, priorities and needs are different from those of your mother. So erase from your mind those "shoulds" and think about what you need to make a system work for you.

If you think about it, you'll probably find that most of your cooking is done from less than 20% of your recipes. It is my observation that the axiom "less is more" is certainly true in the kitchen. The more recipes people have, the fewer they use. And we often spend more time agonizing over the fact we don't use them—or chastising ourselves because we haven't organized them—than we do cooking them! The only solution is to put a stop to this negative cycle.

One common pitfall is to wait to set up a system for today's recipes until you have conquered the backlog of recipes. It will be easier to set up system for the recipes you are collecting now. Then incorporate the backlog into the new system as you have the time, energy and interest.

There are dozens of systems on the market for organizing recipes. If you have found one that suits your needs, by all means use it. But I've found that many of them do not allow for the flexibility that is essential to create a system that is workable for particular situations. For example, the categories may not be the same as you would use, or the space allowed to write, type, or glue the recipe is not large enough.

Keep in mind that this is not a place to let your perfectionism get in the way of starting the task! The system does not need to be perfect, and probably will not be. You can always make adjustments as you experiment.

One of the easiest ways to get started is with manila folders so you can sort your recipes into categories. Designate a place, preferably in or near the kitchen, where you will keep recipes. Put all the supplies you will need there: manila file folders, felt tip pen to label the files,

*The more recipes people have, the fewer they use.*

**Separate the "tried and true" recipes from those you'd like to try.**

scissors, tape, index cards, recipe cards, blank recipe book or whatever system you plan to use.

## Your Recipe Categories

There are dozens of ways to categorize recipes—just compare cookbook indexes, if you doubt it—so don't worry about what categories you want to use. Instead of trying to think up the categories first, start with the recipes you have. Ask yourself, "If I were looking for this recipe, what would I think of?"

As a general rule, start with broader categories first, such as "Bread." Then if the quantity of recipes in that category becomes too bulky to manage, you can subdivide it into "Yeast Breads," "Muffins," "Sweet Breads," etc. If you spend a great deal of time cooking and entertaining and enjoy spending time planning menus, testing new recipes, etc., then you may want your categories to be very specific from the start.

I find it helpful to separate the "tried and true" recipes from those I would like to try. When I'm convinced a recipe is a "winner'—and I don't keep it unless it is—I put it on a 4 x 6 index card and into a card box. The box is divided into categories the same way I divided the recipes in the manila file folders.

The recipes I would like to try stay in the file folders. It is not necessary to type or handwrite the recipe unless you particularly want to. The fastest way is to "cut and paste" the recipe to fit on the index card. You may wish to make notes on the card about when you served it, to whom, what you served with it, or suggestions for adaptations of the recipe.

Decide whether to separate your microwave recipes from your conventional recipes. Many conventional recipes can be adapted to microwave, but many people think of them quite separately.

## The Recipe Search

If you are frequently frustrated because you can't find a recipe from one of your many cookbooks that you used successfully on a previous occasion, put a note that includes the recipe title, cookbook and page number in the appropriate category in your recipe file.

## Computers in the Kitchen

There are a variety of ways you can organize your kitchen with a computer, but the question is whether it will be worth the time and effort. In my experience, in most cases it is not. But if you or a member of your family enjoys entering recipes or keeping track of entertainment records on a computer, go for it!

## Conquering the Recipe Backlog

Once you have a recipe system set up and working, you can decide whether you want to tackle the backlog. You may decide it makes more sense to toss the entire collection.

If you want to incorporate your existing recipes into your system, set aside appropriate time to do it. The amount of time you'll need depends on how much you have and what you think about the project, your working style and circumstances. Will you enjoy the project and want to spend a long time on it? Or will you regard it as a frustrating one for which you will have a limited attention span? Do circumstances dictate that it will be done on a piecemeal basis, even though you would prefer to spend more time at it? Once you have made that decision, write down the commitment to yourself on your calendar.

Is there a family member or friend who will help you? If so, get them involved in the appointment so you will be less likely to ignore it. If organizing the recipes is a major problem for you, hire a professional—"Yes, Virginia, there are people who are good enough, and like it enough, to get paid for organizing recipes."

After you've decided when you're going to conquer the backlog, determine where you will do it. If at all possible, set up a place you can use until the project is completed. (I declared the dining room off limits to the family for two weeks and did it there.) Or set up a card table in the corner of a room. It will be much easier, and

## Action Notes

**Take time when you select a recipe to make a note on your shopping list of the ingredients you'll need to prepare the dish.**

less frustrating, if you don't have to get everything out each time you want to work—and you may find that you will work a few minutes here and there, unplanned, if everything is accessible. My telephone cord stretches into my dining room and I found I could talk on the phone and organize recipes at the same time.

The next step is to collect all the recipes you have—or part of them if looking at them all is too overwhelming—and get organized. Undoubtedly along the way you will get discouraged and overwhelmed. Keep asking yourself these questions: Do I really need this recipe? Does it exist somewhere else? How long has it been since I've used, or had, the recipe? What's the worst possible thing that would happen if I tossed it? As you sort, you may well discover that your standards change as you realize how much work is involved to keep everything you had planned to keep.

### Trying New Recipes

One of the essential steps in keeping the recipes in your kitchen under control is developing a method for trying new ones. Whenever I begin to feel like I'm in a cooking rut or if I have some extra time, I choose six to eight recipes I would like to try in the next few weeks. Usually I pick one or two main dishes, one or two salads or vegetables, one or two soups, and one or two desserts.

When you've selected the new recipes you want to try, take time to note on your shopping list the ingredients you will need to prepare these dishes. Then clip the recipes to a magnet on the refrigerator or put them in a special compartment in your recipe box or book. When you are rushed to get dinner on the table but want to try something new you will have the menu idea and the ingredients right at your finger tips. (The same technique can be used in choosing recipes that your children can prepare if they cook while you are working.)

The final step in this system is making a decision about the recipe after you have eaten the results. Was it great? If not, why keep it? Avoid the "I really should give it one more try" syndrome. There are undoubtedly thousands more recipes you can try that might be great, so let it go! Then your recipe collection becomes something you really treasure instead of tolerate.

One winter I was snowbound for four days. I had a wonderful time experimenting with my new recipes. In addition, I had a freezer full of food that could be microwaved for a speedy nutritious meal on the days following the snow when I was too busy catching up on lost time to spend time cooking.

*Avoid the "I really should give it one more try" syndrome.*

## Entertainment Records

**A** client of mine had invited a certain gentleman to her home on several occasions with various dinner guests. She was most embarrassed to discover that she had served tomatoes stuffed with spinach on the last three occasions! (Unfortunately, he didn't like it the first time!)

One way to avoid that problem is to create a notebook to record your entertaining. Just as with the recipes, there are various ways to organize this notebook. If you entertain lavishly and frequently have the same guests, it will require more time to maintain the system than if you entertain simply and/or infrequently. The simplest way is to list the events in chronological order. Include the menu, table decorations, guest list (and seating arrangement, if you wish), and perhaps even what you wore. It is also helpful to list suggestions you have on any improvements you might want to make when you entertain again, whether it is a slight change in a recipe (which should be noted on your recipe card or in your recipe book), a suggestion about serving logistics (for example, the coffee should be on a separate table or serve small forks with the appetizers), or a note about the flowers.

If you entertain frequently and are particularly concerned about not duplicating menus for the same guests, you could put a separate alphabetical section in your book. Each guest would have a small section where you could put the date when you entertained him/her. Then

**If you usually shop at the same store, make up a checklist in categories arranged in the order of the store's aisles.**

you could check the chronological list for the menu that guest was served. For example, under "A', you would have: "Adams, John—3/6/90; 10/2/90; 5/4/91; etc. You could also note there any items of concern when entertaining that guest—allergies, food preferences, medical concerns, etc.

## To Market, To Market

A major issue is keeping track of the food we have on hand and the food we need to purchase. I find it helpful to have a shopping list posted on the refrigerator, with a pencil permanently attached with a string.

There are paper-management techniques you can use to simplify your shopping trips. For example, if you do the majority of your shopping in the same store, create a checklist of the items you most frequently purchase, arranged in the order of the grocery store aisles. Leave space in each section for special items that are not regularly on the list.

Make a dozen copies. After you've tried the system that many times, you will probably identify ways you want to change the form. You may decide to post the form itself on the refrigerator door to check off items as you go, or, if there are family members who are unable or unwilling to use the list, it may be easier to transfer the ad hoc list from the refrigerator onto the form just before you go to the store.

If you have problems with people forgetting to put items on the list when they use the last of something, try making a list of commonly used items. Then, just before you do a major shopping, you can make a quick check to see which of those items are low in supply.

## Coupon Coordination

A discussion of papers in the kitchen would not be complete without including the issue of coupons. Decision-making and organization, in that order, are the keys to saving with manufacturers coupons and refund offers.

The first decision to make is whether you are really serious or committed to the idea of coupon clipping. My personal opinion is that unless you enjoy doing it or your budget requires it coupon saving is too much trouble. Ask yourself, "Do I really save money when I consider the time it takes me? Do I end up buying more expensive products that I would not necessarily buy if I did not have the coupon? Is clipping coupons an attempt to assuage my guilt feelings over excess spending habits, or an effort to appease my mother?" One man I know looks at coupon clipping as a game and uses it for relaxation.

Many people I know clip only coupons worth 35 cents or more, and they clip only those for products they routinely buy, such as coffee, laundry soap and paper products. Other people spend two to three hours a week clipping and can save $30-$50 per week on grocery purchases, in addition to the amount received in cash from rebate offers. I read in a newspaper about one woman who bought $113.05 worth of groceries for $1.69. The real price: Her office is a corner of the basement, where she has organized coupons, labels and proofs of purchases into 14 grocery bags, six cardboard boxes, eight filing-cabinet drawers and a bookcase! "This kind of couponing is available to anyone who is willing to get organized," she said, peering over the mountain of groceries in her cart.

To organize coupons, the basic principle, "put like things together," certainly applies. Establish categories for your coupons in the same way you establish categories for your recipes. Ask the question, "If I wanted this coupon, what category would I think of?"

There are several possibilities for categories, such as "Paper Products," "Cleaning Products," and "Vegetables" (this could be broken down in "Vegetables—Frozen," and "Vegetables—Canned'). In addition, you may want a separate system for refunds. It could be located in the same container, but in a separate section. Within that system, you would have the same categories as you had

*Do you really want to be seriously committed to the idea of coupon clipping?*

for coupons. In addition, you might want a section for "Refunds in Progress."

Keep a supply of return-address labels, envelopes and stamps on hand. For a refund offer that requires several proof of purchase labels, put the labels in a pre-addressed envelope that has the refund expiration date on the top right-hand corner.

The technique you use for storing coupons is also important. Decide whether you will always carry all your coupons with you when you go to the store or whether you will have a "Master Coupon Box" at home from which you can pull out those coupons you want to take with you. While at the store, you can use a regular business-sized envelope (or several) or you can purchase a "Coupon Billfold" designed specifically for that purpose. It is unlikely that the categories in a pre-designed system will be the same as yours, so feel free to put on your own labels to make the system work for you. However you choose to keep the coupons, be sure to purge expired coupons on a regular basis.

One woman I know divides her coupons according to the shopping aisles in her local store. Not only does the system add continuity to her coupon and refund hobby, but it saves her an incredible amount of time.

Experiment until you find a method that works for you. There is no right or wrong decision on this issue. Just decide, recognizing that you can change your decision at any time based on your current circumstances. Once your decision is made, concentrate on setting up the system needed to make the decision workable. But above all, create a system that gives you a feeling of success!

# Children and Paper

**C**hildren and paper go hand-in-hand in our society. As soon as a couple even begins to think about starting a family, the paper begins to accumulate—information on childbirth classes, ads from childcare services, notices of "mother's day out" programs, descriptions of child-rearing techniques, articles on overcoming fertility problems, and books about the psychological impact of parenting and the "how tos" of surviving parenthood.

*It is essential to involve your children in the selection process from the beginning.*

*Teaching paper-management skills to children also teaches decision-making skills they'll need for life.*

There are numerous approaches to surviving this paper blizzard, but the first and most important step is to start some kind of system. As your children grow older, the system will need to change, but you don't need to worry about that now.

## For the Parent-to-Be

The first step toward establishing a system that will work for you is to examine your own feelings about keeping and using information. Is it important to you to have easy access to articles about childrearing or would you be more likely to ask your doctor, a psychologist or discuss it with your parents or a friend? Do you need the information near you to feel secure, even if you never use it? Or does having paper around create additional stress, guilt or frustration? Is it realistic that you will take the time and effort required to maintain an extensive library or is there someone else in the family who will help you? These are important questions to answer to prevent setting unrealistic standards for yourself. You create a "no-win" situation if you feel guilty because you keep too much, and feel guilty if you don't! Eliminate the "shoulds," and acknowledge what will work for you.

## Collect and Categorize

The simplest way to begin any system is to collect all the information you have into the largest general category. In this case, that's "Children." Find a container, a basket, shelf or file and label it clearly.

When there is more information than can be easily handled and the file becomes too bulky, divide the information into the next logical categories. For example, information about children can be categorized into areas of concern such as education, medical, memorabilia, legal information, and toys and equipment. Notice that "toys and equipment" are put together; it is often too difficult to differentiate between the categories. However, you may have "Toys and Equipment—Owned" and "Toys and Equipment—Shopping Information."

One of the facts about paper management is that our needs are constantly changing. A system that works when a child is six months old might be totally inappropriate when she is sixteen, and the system that works when she is sixteen will be overkill when she is twenty.

For example, when your child is in elementary school, a file labeled "Susan—Education" may be sufficient. However, when she enters high school that category may be too general. The categories you will need at this point depend on your particular style and on your child's interests. If you are very active in your educational program, you may need a file for "PTA," "College Preparation," or "Extracurricular Activities." (That last catetogy might need to be subdivided into "Gymnastics," "Scouts," etc.) And when your child has gone off to college, many of these files will no longer be necessary. At this point all the report cards for kindergarten through high school become highly irrelevant. Choose one or two for your grandchildren to see.

If you want to keep all the files about your child together, put the child's name at the beginning of each label: "Susan—Education," "Susan—Sports," for example.

If you know that you will not take the time to develop a detailed filing system, find a basket, shelf or file and label it "John—Education." It may take you 10 minutes to go through the entire box if you need a copy of an award certificate to go with a college application, but it will be a massive improvement over having all the members of the family turning the house upside down looking for that large brown envelope!

## Teach Your Children Well

With all the obligations and options in today's world, it is very easy for a parent to spend an inordinate amount of time being a social secretary, or just a "nag-ger." Teaching your child organizational skills will bene-fit you and your child—for life!

One of the biggest problems we all face is making choices. Over and over I find houses buried in paper be-cause adults feel compelled to do it all—read every book, newspaper and magazine, keep every photo and memen-to, or go to every concert, seminar and reception. Living a happy and healthy life, or even just coping, in today's world means making choices. Remember, clutter is post-poned decisions. As parents we should teach that concept to our children, and one place to begin is with paper.

There are many steps you can take to help your children learn how to manage the paper in their lives, as well as to become good time managers.

As soon as your child goes into an organized play-group or educational program, you will begin to accumu-late paper. Designate a special place for her to put the papers she brings home from school. If you start this habit early, you will avoid many panic situations of try-ing to find a trip permission slip when you should be getting ready for work or running out the door to catch the car pool. Each evening or first thing in the morning you can check and see what came home from school and what requires your attention.

## The Art Pile

One of the major issues in managing your child's papers is dealing with the creative papers she brings home. Young children can produce enough paper to fill a small art gallery within a week. The big question is which of those 400 finger-painted gems will become cher-ished examples of the early works of upcoming Picassos.

There is nothing wrong with keeping everything that our children create if we have plenty of space to keep it, and plenty of energy to organize it. But few people have either. It is easy to get caught in the trap of feeling guilty if we throw away the things our children make, and feeling overwhelmed if we don't. It is essential to involve your children in the selection process from the beginning.

You can use this process as a tool for teaching them decision-making techniques, which will be important for them to know as they grow up. All the papers you would like to keep can be put in a basket, or on a bulletin board with your child's name prominently displayed. Then when the basket gets full or the bulletin board gets crowded, encourage Susan to choose her three favorite papers, which can be put in a Memorabilia Box for safekeeping. Put the child's name, age, and date on the back of the artwork to make it more meaningful 20 years from now.

There are other creative uses for artwork. Put several creations together and make a collage for your child's wall or to use as a present for a relative. Grandparents, aunts and uncles are delighted to receive letters from children. Have your child write a short message on the back of the painting, or just send the painting— signed, of course! Teach your child the value of recycling. Artwork makes wonderful wrapping paper for gifts to take to birthday parties.

**When the bulletin board gets crowded, encourage your child to choose a few favorite papers and put them in a memorabilia box for safekeeping.**

## Kids and Calendars

As your children get older, there are many other steps you can take to help them learn how to manage their paper and to improve their time-management skills. For example, put a large calendar with plenty of writing space in an easily accessible place. The refrigerator is frequently a good choice, because everyone ends up there sooner or later!

Have each child note when he or she needs transportation to basketball, cookies for a school party, or plans to spend the night at a friend's house. This method helps you plan your schedule and avoids last-minute crises. If Sam comes running to you at the last minute and says, "Mom, I need a ride to gymnastics," you can

**"Letting go" is a life skill.**

say, "I didn't see it on the calendar, Son, and I can't take you right now." If he misses an important practice or is late for his game, it won't take him long to realize that he has to take some responsibility for his own life. Obviously, you have to take into account unusual circumstances and make exceptions when you feel it is appropriate to do so.

Don't forget that you owe the same courtesy to your children. For the career parent, this is a great place to communicate facts about your schedule that will affect your son or daughter. Include travel schedules, night meetings or houseguests. Consider using different colored pens for each member of the family, and attach the pens with a long string next to the calendar so you won't hear the excuse "I couldn't find a pencil!"

As soon as Johnny begins getting school assignments in advance, help him choose an assignment book. Teach him how to plot out complicated assignments by reading one-half chapter each day—or if it works better to read two chapters at a time, choose those days on which there are not other obligations such as piano lessons or soccer practice. Discuss the concept of choosing styles. Remind him to watch for family commitments that might affect his schedule. Recognize that his style may not be the same as yours, but that does not mean it is wrong.

Encourage your children to use a calendar for keeping track of sports events, babysitting commitments, job responsibilities at home, birthdays they want to remember, etc.

The calendar is also an excellent place to help your child understand the importance of goal setting. If, for example, Susan *really* wants to take a trip this summer that you feel is too expensive, or you feel she should contribute to the cost, help her plan how she could make it happen by using the calendar. Count the number of weeks until she needs the money and determine how much she will have to make every week if she is to succeed. She can use the calendar to block out time when she will work and set goals for raising the money.

## *Your Child's Own Files*

**A**s your child gets older, help him organize the papers he needs to cope with daily life. Purchase several file folders and help label them according to his needs. Make a category for each subject at school and each area of interest. At the end of the year encourage and assist your child, if necessary, in cleaning out the file and determining what papers he would like to keep as mementos, and which have served their purpose and can be thrown away.

If your children are involved in several organizations, a file called "Directories" can be very useful to keep the lists of participant's names that you receive from scouts, sports, school, youth group, etc. This file can save many hassles when Saturday morning rolls around and you are madly trying to find a ride to soccer for your child. The information is also helpful if your child is sending out party invitations or trying to locate a friend's phone number or address.

My 15-year-old son stopped in my office one day and noticed on my desk an X-Rack—a plastic frame designed to hold hanging file folders. He's a "gadget lover" and interested in art. He asked if I would get him one. The combination of the uniqueness of the file holder and the bright-colored file folders with plastic tabs fascinated him—and gave me a terrific opening to help him in setting up a file system for his needs. It is very important to do whatever you can to make the organizing process appeal to your child. It's a great way to create one-on-one time, and you benefit doubly because both you and your child's lives will run more smoothly.

Your child may also want files that relate to special interests. For example, your teenager might want a category on "Fashion" or "Shopping Ideas" to take on your next shopping trip.

Be sure your child makes a file index or list of the files to keep in the very front of the files. For an example of one 19-year-old's file categories, see the box in the margin at right.

---

### A 19-Year-Old's File Index

Car
Carnegie
  Mellon-general
Carnegie
  Mellon-courses,
  grades, loan
Computer languages
Employment-
  paycheck stuff,
  rules
Finance-bank
  account, canceled
  checks
Legal
  Stuff-leases/credit
  card info
Medical
NASA
Resume
Stories
Taxes
Utilities
Video games
Writing/papers

# CHAPTER

# TWENTY
# ONE

# Travel and Papers

*If you travel
frequently, make a
standard packing list.*

**A** primary example of how paperwork has multi-plied in our modern world is found in the area of travel: bonus programs for airline travel, car rentals and hotel accommodations. Entire books have been written, newsletters published and computer software designed to make it easier for the traveler to take advantage of all the offers. Not taking advantage of such offers cre-ates the same kind of emotion in us as not submitting

our medical expenses to the insurance company for re-imbursement!

## *All That Paraphernalia*

Travel brings with it other kinds of paper problems as well: maps, directions, confirmations, tickets, itineraries, notes about people to see and things to do, papers we need to take with us on the trip, addresses and phone numbers, traveler's checks, passports and all the identification cards with numbers you need to get credit for those fabulous bonus programs.

Then there are all the papers you collect while you are traveling: more maps, phone numbers and addresses of new friends made, favorite restaurants and shops, receipts for purchases that are being shipped to you, boarding passes and ticket stubs, travel brochures and a variety of memorabilia.

If your trip involved any meetings, you will undoubtedly have a pile of papers that contain all kinds of wonderful information you want to keep or use.

You arrive home from the trip with the best of intentions about going through all those papers, but as soon as you walk in the door you are confronted with all the mail that arrived while you were away. So it is likely that the trip papers are pushed aside so you can deal with more pressing matters. After several weeks, you get tired of looking at them or you have company coming and need to clear off the table, so into a drawer they go, never to be seen again!

Do you cut out travel articles? Collect travel magazines or reviews about travel books? In order for them to be useful to you, you need to organize them. When was the last time you went through a pile of old magazines to find that article about the terrific restaurant in San Francisco?

Let's take a look at the various areas and see what can be done to manage the travel-related paper in our lives.

### Family Fun

If you or your family enjoy taking day trips but have difficulty thinking where to go on the spur of the moment, create a "Day Trip Ideas" file. Information in the file can also help when you have house guests. "Vacation Ideas" can also be a useful file when it is time to decide on a summer vacation plan.

*Keep your monthly mileage statements as long as you participate in the program because airlines sometimes offer special bonuses to travelers who have accumulated a certain number of miles during a certain length of time.*

## Essential Information

First of all, consider the travel information you want to keep for reference. This would include maps, travel brochures, information from past trips, newsletters from travel services and bonus programs information. The first step is to get all the information together. If you have a small amount, you may need something as simple as a file or box labeled "Travel Information." But if you have more than will fit into one category comfortably you need to decide how to organize the information. One way would be to group it by category. Make a pile for maps, another for airline information, another for travel brochures, etc. These could then be incorporated into your reference file under "Travel," so the labels would look like this: "Travel—Airline Information," "Travel—Brochures," "Travel—Receipts," etc.

For the frequent traveler, this system will still need refining. For example, if you participate in several frequent flyer programs, you will need a separate file for each airline, so you would have a series of files such as "Airlines—American," "Airlines—United," "Airlines—Delta," etc.

If your immediate reaction is horror at the thought of so many files, consider this. Suppose you're rushing out of the door to grab a flight. The last thing in the world you need to do is go through a pile of papers from an airline you are not taking. It will take only a second to grab the information from the appropriate airline file. (You might also find it helpful to put frequent flyer information on your rotary phone-file, along with the phone numbers of the airlines.)

You will soon discover that your airline files become bulky very quickly, so it is important to establish your retention guidelines. I would suggest you keep your monthly mileage statements for as long as you participate in the program because airlines sometimes offer special bonuses to travelers who have accumulated a certain number of miles during a certain length of time. Most airlines send a monthly newsletter. Keep only the latest one, unless there is specific information in an older newsletter. If so, mark clearly what information interests you so that you quickly identify why you kept that particular newsletter.

This same system will work for hotel and car-rental bonus programs. Of course, the most important information to have is your membership number.

One of the other complicating factors in this issue are the "Tie-in Programs." For example, certain airlines have reciprocal privileges. Or, if you fly one airline and rent your car from a tie-in agency, you can get bonus miles. There are several books and newsletters on the market that describe these offers. If you are serious about collecting bonus points, one of them would be worth your investment.

## *Maps and Brochures*

**M**aps can be another paper problem for the traveler. If you have only a dozen or so maps, one file or box will be plenty, but if you have more than that refine your system by geographic area. I started with "U.S.—Northeast," "U.S.—Northwest," "U.S.—Southeast," "U.S.—Southwest." As my travel increased dramatically, I now have one file for every state and several for foreign countries.

What about travel brochures? To determine how these should be filed, you need to identify why you are keeping them at all. The answer might not be the same for each brochure. You may be keeping one strictly as a memento of a beautiful experience, another as a reference in case you return, or another to share with a friend. Ask yourself, "Under what circumstances would I want this information?" The answer will help you determine where you should file it. Put a date on the brochure when you file it so it will be easier to clean out the files in the years to come.

If you have more than eight to 10 travel files, I

*Travel information is dated quickly. Is it recent enough to be useful?*

**As soon as you begin planning for any trip, make a file with the destination on the label.**

suggest you create a separate filing system for travel, rather than incorporating them into your existing files. Identify travel files with a particular color so you can recognize them easily.

## Before the Trip

As soon as you begin planning for any trip, make a file with the destination on the label, such as "New York." This will provide an immediate place to put any information regarding the trip—tickets, itinerary, reminders of things you want to take with you, contacts you want to make while you are there, or places you want to visit or shop. If you travel frequently, you may have several trip files at one time.

If you travel frequently, make a standard packing list. Keep it in your "To Do" Book or in your suitcase. Then as soon as you begin planning a trip, take the list and put it in the destination file. As you think of things you want to take with you, note them on the packing list.

When you pack your suitcase, check off each item and note the specific number taken. For example, "Dress Shirts—6." (One client puts her list in a plastic folder and uses a grease pencil to check it off. Then it can be easily erased after each use.) If you are concerned about losing your luggage and being able to substantiate a claim, keep the list until you return from the trip.

People who travel with children can use the list to help their children get everything repacked in the suitcase. When my daughter was twelve, she decided to take the list with her so that when she was repacking her suitcase, she could check it off to be sure she remembered to bring everything home with her.

Make a "Pre-trip Checklist" to remind you of last-minute tasks that are easy to forget, such as "Check thermostat," "Turn off coffeepot," "Stop newspaper," and "Arrange for plant and pet care."

If you have filed your travel reference material by geographical area, it will be very easy to check that file for any additional information you might want on a particular trip. Sometimes I even take the file with me for airplane reading. Be sure to take a list of frequent flyer numbers. These could be listed in your "To Do" Book under "Travel" or "Numbers."

## On the Trip

If you are going to attend any kind of meeting while you're on the trip and will be collecting a number of papers, I suggest you create action files for the trip. It will be easier to make decisions about what you want to do with the papers as you acquire them than it will be to go back through the papers when you return home. These action files might include "Write," "File," "Hold." (See Chapter 10).

What about travel receipts? You cannot decide what to do with a receipt unless you identify why it is useful to you. Do you need it to prove a tax deductible expense? If so, it could go with other tax information for the year. (See Chapter 14.) Are you keeping it until the china that you purchased arrives safely? If so, it could go in a "To Hold" file (See Chapter 10.) When the china arrives, the receipt could go in a "Personal Property" file in case you need it to substantiate an insurance claim.

## After the Trip

When the trip is over, put your ticket stub and boarding passes in the airline file until you are certain your miles have been credited to your account. Then throw the boarding passes away. File the ticket stub only if you need it for a specific reason—for example, a business reimbursement or a tax deductible expense. Otherwise, throw it away.

Take action on any papers you have brought home with you or incorporate them into your existing action files.

*When the trip is over, keep your ticket stub and boarding passes in the appropriate airline file until you're certain your miles have been credited to your frequent-flyer account.*

Finally, be sure to purge the trip file itself. Throw away any information that is no longer relevant and file the remaining information into the appropriate file.

Suppose, for example, you meet someone on a trip who lives in another city you visit frequently, or hope to visit one day. Put her name and address with a note about where you met in that geographical file. Does all this sound like too much drudgery? It may be a lifesaver if you find yourself stranded in her city one day, or just a lot of fun if you get together and reminisce about all the fun you had on that Caribbean cruise!

CHAPTER

TWENTY
TWO

# Home Computers and Paper

**T**here are many books on the subject of personal computers. This is not the place for a major discussion about them, but it would be foolish to write a book on paper management in this day and age without mentioning personal computers. They can, without a doubt, do many miraculous things to help us manage our lives more effectively. They will not, however, solve a paper-management problem.

Some People Love Computers Because They Can Cut Down on Paper Clutter.

**A personal computer can complicate paper management considerably because it's so easy to create more paper.**

In fact, if a personal computer is used improperly it can complicate paper management considerably because it's so easy to create more paper. For example, you write a letter or a report and print out a copy to edit it. When you have completed the editing and entered the changes in the computer, you print out another copy. Within minutes you have doubled the amount of paper in your life.

## Too Many Printouts

The computer will not make decisions for you. For example, people who have computers with programs that print special reports, especially home account systems, often feel compelled to print out every report possible to ensure that they are getting the most out of their computer. What they often get is confused!

This is also a major reason that paper gets out of hand. The best approach is to print one of each report the first time or two you use a new program. Then study the reports and determine which ones are useful to you, and print only those. Keep in mind that any paper is of extremely limited value to you if you cannot identify specifically why you are keeping it. Ask yourself that familiar question, "Under what circumstances would I use this information?" This not only cuts down on the amount of paper, it also cuts down on the amount of confusion.

Store printed computer reports in your filing system whenever possible. For reports too large for the system, use binders to make the papers easier to manage and refer to. Label the binder as to contents and date. This will speed up the purging process considerably and will make the binders easier to access while they are still useful.

## Make Your Computer Work for You

A computer can simplify many of your paper-management tasks. The computer is an excellent tool for maintaining a File Index. However, you will find it helpful to print out two copies—one to keep in front of your files and another at your desk. Make entries and deletions by hand, and then periodically update it on the computer.

There are programs designed to replace or supplement your calendar and your "To Do" list. These programs are becoming more popular with the advent of more portable notebook computers.

You can even organize your recipes. But before you take that step, be sure the results will be worth the time and energy it will take to enter the data in your computer and to maintain it.

On the other hand, the "sort" capabilities of a computer can be a real boost to your rotary phone-file and eliminate the problem of whether to list Peter Pipewrench under "Plumber," "Household repairs," or "Pipewrench, Peter."

There are numerous software packages for managing your finances. It is important, however, that you know what information you need. If you couldn't decide what information to put in a budget book, a computer may not solve the problem.

Even if you decide not to use a complete money-management package, you can use your word-processing program for keeping track of numerous records. For example, if you are frustrated keeping track of membership and subscription records, you can list all of them in alphabetical order, with the date you renewed and for how long. The next time you get a bill for a magazine, pull up your list on the screen and you will know how long before the subscription actually expires. The same system works well for keeping track of charitable donations.

## Computer Copy Versus Hard Copy

Many people believe that it must be preferable to keep documents in their computer rather than in their filing system. But consider this: If I have 100 documents in hard copy and you have the same 100 documents in the computer—or on floppy disks—which of us will find a particular document more quickly? If most cases, I will. It takes time to scroll down your computer screen to bring up each one of those documents.

My recommendation is to use your computer to store documents that you will be updating or using again. However, for "one-time documents" such as a thank you letter or a memo, keep a copy in your reference files and then only if you might want to refer to it. (See Chapter 11.)

## *Organizing Your Computer Documents*

**H**ave you ever sat in front of your computer scrolling up and down the screen looking for a particular document you entered a few months ago, last week—or even yesterday! And heaven forbid if someone else entered it and you are trying to find it!

Most word-processing programs are designed so that you can create directories and subdirectories. You can use the same principle to organize your computer documents in your computer as you do your hard-copy documents in your filing cabinet. For example, I have directories in my computer for personal interests such as "Church," "Family" and "Journal," as well as directories for professional categories such as "Advertising," "Articles I've Written" (divided into subdirectories called "Education," "Medical," "Personal," etc.), "Fees," "Forms," "Overheads," "Outlines," "Procedures," "Promo," "Quotes," "Speeches," "Surveys," "Video."

I make an index of the directories and subdirectories, just as I do my reference files, and keep a hard copy near the computer. Then, when I'm working on a document and want to decide where to store it, I refer to the index instead of roaming through the computer trying to determine where the document should go.

You can also organize computer files with floppy disks. Categorize the information on disks the same way you would categorize them on a hard-disk drive or as you would hard copy in folders in a reference file system. For example, I have separate disks for "Advertising," "Fees," "Speeches," etc.

## Computer Clean-Up

The same purging principles apply to your computer that apply to your paper files. Set up a regular schedule for cleaning out your computer files—even more frequently than you clean your paper files. In addition, each time I pull up a directory to add a new document, I do a quick check to see if there is an old one I can erase, or perhaps take out of the hard-disk system and store on a floppy disk if I think I'll need it in the future. Most of the time there is!

## Another Recycling Opportunity

Recycle your used computer paper. Use the backside for drafts. Cut it into various sizes to use as scratch paper beside your telephones and in the kitchen. If you prefer pads, you can take the paper to a commercial printer and have it cut and padded into handy scratch pads for a small charge. (And, of course, there is always the bottom of the bird cage!)

*Set up a regular schedule for cleaning out your computer files.*

CHAPTER

TWENTY
THREE

# "Paperholics"

*People who have the most difficulty managing paper are often the people who generate the most paper.*

**W**hile paper management for most of us is something we can live with, for others it is an insurmountable struggle. Their daily lives are seriously hampered, and in some cases brought to a standstill, by the endless clutter of unfinished projects, unread newspapers, magazines and books, unanswered mail and unfiled paper in unidentified piles, bags, and boxes throughout the house. I call these people "paperholics."

Each individual may feel his or her situation is unique, but thousands of people experience the same distress. For some, this constant stress can lead to physical ailments. Some paperholics live in fear of being discovered and go to great lengths to avoid having friends and relatives come to their homes. Some even close off parts of their houses. Others cover up their embarrassment with humorous signs like "A clean desk is a sign of a sick mind," or "Enter at your own risk!"

Many paperholics end up paying unnecessary service charges and tax penalties or having their household utilities cut off because they could not find or complete the paperwork. Paperholics constantly make excuses for their behavior or deny it entirely. Some rarely go anywhere because they cannot enjoy themselves until their paperwork is finished. Others never stay at home to avoid facing the chaos. Marriage and family relationships suffer seriously when the paperholic's clutter intrudes on others.

## Who Are the Paperholics?

Paperholics can be people of any age. A paperholic is someone to whom every piece of paper represents an opportunity, an obligation, a threat, a memory or a dream. Paperholics keep piles of articles in case they need to prove a position on a particular issue. They hold on to newspapers because they haven't had time to read or clip the articles. (The irony is that usually they cannot find the articles when they want them; sometimes they do not even realize that they have them.)

There is nothing wrong with keeping every greeting card and letter you've ever received, if you have plenty of space and it brings you pleasure. If, however, your daily living is impeded because of papers out of the past, you need to examine your actions. The reason and degree of attachment and the ability to let go due to new circumstances distinguishes between normal and pathological saving. Psychologists have studied people referred to as

*A paperholic is someone to whom every piece of paper represents an opportunity, an obligation, a threat, a memory or a dream.*

## Real Life Paperholics

•An internationally recognized medical researcher asked me to help organize his office. When I arrived, we literally rolled piles of paper out of his office on his chair to make room for me to stand!

•A woman called and told me she hadn't had anyone in her home for over 10 years. The reason? Paper piled on every flat surface, stuffed in shopping bags under the bed and shoved in all available drawer and cupboard space. Her children tried to help, but every attempt turned into an emotional disaster. The situation came to a head when the condominium management called the fire department.

"packrats." They believe that, for some, the problem is a result of an early childhood trauma—a significant loss of some kind. For many people, the problem became out of control because of extenuating circumstances such as ill health, renovating or moving, family crisis, loss of job, etc. All the causes of this behavior are not clearly identified, but most savers are not pathological hoarders.

People who have the most difficulty managing paper are often the people who generate the most paper. They feel compelled to make duplicate copies so they will be sure to find at least one. Many order information booklets from every available source—even on subjects that may not relate to their lives. They tend to take advantage of every offer for a free magazine issue, fully intending to cancel the subscription later. They take copious notes on any available piece of paper. They pick up information brochures and articles wherever they go. They often subscribe to more magazines and newspapers than they could ever possibly read—and end up reading few of them.

In the end, paperholics live in a vicious cycle. The more paper they accumulate, the less able they are to manage it, and the more out of control they feel.

## If You Are a Paperholic

First of all it is essential that you admit you have a problem. Recognize that change does not happen instantaneously. Shelves overflowing with books and outdated magazines, boxes of paper and paper-shuffling habits accumulated over years won't disappear overnight. Behavior patterns take time to relearn. Paper-management skills do not come naturally to everyone.

Accept the fact that you cannot undo what you may now feel are mistakes. Take the advice in this book with the idea of starting over with today's papers. Ignore the backlog for now. Create a place to work that you find pleasant. Set up your paper-management center (as described in Chapter 3) to handle today's paper. Keep asking yourself the question, "What is the worst possible thing that would happen if I didn't have this piece of paper?" Begin to imagine how you will feel when you are successful. What will your house look like? What things will you do that you aren't doing now?

Even if you read all the guidelines in this book, if you are a true paperholic it is unlikely that you will make the dramatic changes you want to make without assistance of some kind. It is essential to find people you trust to help you. Here are several possibilities:

- A self-help support group in your area. Two excellent organizations that offer newsletters, publications, and information about support groups are:

  Messies Anonymous
  5025 S.W. 114th Avenue
  Miami, FL 33165
  305-271-8404

  Packrats International
  12662 Hoover Street
  Garden Grove, CA 92641
  714-894-8223

- A mental-health professional to help you deal with such psychological issues as why you need to hang on to all that paper.
- An organizing consultant who will work with you to go through the paper piece by piece. (Chapter 24 has more information.)
- A very special nonjudgmental friend or relative who will work with you or encourage and support you. (I must add that such a person is often not easy to find.)
- A combination of any or all of the above.

## If Someone You Love Is a Paperholic

If someone you know or love is a paperholic, you may be asking "What can I do?" Truthfully, maybe

### More real-life stories

- An elementary school teacher wrote that his entire house, as well as his work area at school, was filled with paper. The thought of throwing anything away made him feel physically ill.

- One woman told me she had moved out of her apartment and into a new one. Not unusual, except that she kept the old one for the purpose of storing all of her paper!

- A client slept on the sofa in his living room because the twin beds in his bedroom were covered with the papers he had accumulated after his wife died.

- Another client had files full of vacation ideas but he had not left the city for more than two days in over 10 years.

*There is nothing wrong with keeping every greeting card and letter you've ever received, if you have plenty of space and it brings you pleasure.*

nothing. It's easy for us to be critical of others who find it difficult to do what we do easily, and it's important to accept that correcting the situation will require much more than simply applying self-discipline.

Sometimes letting a paperholic know that other people have similar difficulties can be a great relief. One of the most common reactions to the scenarios I present in paper-management seminars is, "When did you see my house?"

Perhaps the most important lesson I have learned about living with a paperholic is the importance of defining boundaries. If possible, negotiate with that person regarding what papers (magazines, newspapers, photos, etc.) are acceptable in shared spaces. Identify other areas of your home where he or she can accumulate paper according to his or her own wishes. When the papers begin to spill into other areas, you have a right to take steps to correct the problem. Communication is a key issue. Often it takes time and practice, as well as professional assistance, to master effective techniques.

Finally, acknowledge that all of us have issues we need to resolve. Concentrate on your own issues and allow the paperholic to solve his or her own problem.

CHAPTER

TWENTY
FOUR

# Caging That Tiger

At this point, a review of the basic components of this paper-management system is in order. Keep in mind that every piece of paper in your life can be categorized into one of seven categories:

- "To Sort" Tray
- Wastebasket
- Calendar
- "To Do" List

*The key issue in any paper-management system is decision making.*

- Rotary phone-file/Phone Book
- Action Files
- Reference Files

Every time you find a pile of papers that require decisions, ask yourself these questions about each piece:

- "Can this be recycled or go in the wastebasket?"
- If not, "Do I need to make an appointment with myself to do something?" If so, enter the information in your calendar.
- "Does this piece of paper require action or recall by me at some yet-undetermined time in the future?" If so, enter it in your "To Do" list.
- "Are there any addresses, telephone numbers, or pieces of "mini information" that I should put on my rotary phone-file or in my computer database?"
- If you entered the information in any of the above places, "Do I still need to keep the piece of paper?" If so, "Does this piece of paper require action or am I keeping it for reference?"
- If it requires action, "What specific action do I need to take?" The answer will tell you into which Action File you should put it.
- If I am keeping it for reference, "What word would I think of if I wanted this piece of paper again?" The answer will tell you into what Reference File you should put it.

## Getting Rid of the Boxes

In the question and answer period following one of my speeches, a woman asked, "I have four large packing boxes full of papers that I have been telling myself for three years I will organize 'one of these days,' but each time I try I am totally overwhelmed. What can I do?"

I told her that I could think of only two options for getting rid of the boxes: Decide that since she survived for three years without any of the information in them she could take a deep breath and toss them all in the trash; or go through the papers one by one using the system described in this book, making decisions on each piece of paper.

You have the same choices for dealing with your accumulated papers. It may help you determine which option you want to choose to know that going through the equivalent of one vertical-file cabinet drawer takes about four hours. If the peace of mind you will get from going through the papers is worth four hours of your time, by all means make an appointment with yourself to do it as soon as possible. If spending that time in some other way is more important, then throw the boxes away immediately. If you find yourself postponing the decision, ask yourself, "What am I going to know tomorrow that I don't know today?"

## Just Get Started

At this point, one of the major questions you may have is "How long will it take?" You cannot expect to solve all of your paper-management problems overnight. Don't worry how long it will take. Just get started. One of the most exciting things you will discover is that what you learn in organizing one area of your life will carry over into other areas. As you enjoy your successes, you will be encouraged to keep going.

## Keep It Growing

There are no magic wands! No matter how terrific the system you develop, it will not maintain itself, and it will not last forever. If after reading this book, or even parts of it, you have to admit that you are not willing to do what needs to be done, then your assignment is to determine who will help you and how.

Keep in mind, however, that the key issue in any paper-management system is decision making. You will either have to make the decisions yourself, or give the

**Action Notes**

person to whom you delegate your paper management the authority to make those decisions. A successful system will probably require a combination of decision making and delegation.

Many times a client will call me because a system they have established is not working. Nine times out of 10, the problem is not that the system was bad but that they have outgrown the system. Personal paper management is an ongoing process. It will need to change as you change. If your priorities, your support system, your space availability or your family situation change, you may need to adjust your system to fit those changes.

## *Call for Action*

If you have read this book and still don't know how to create an effective system or want additional support or assistance for your specific needs, check your local yellow pages under "Organizing Consultants" or "Personal Services" and find someone who specializes in setting up systems for paper management. Write to NAPO (National Association for Professional Organizers, 1163 Shermer Road, Northbrook, IL 60062-4538. Or call 708-272-0135 for a list of organizers in your area.

Many people procrastinate about making an appointment with an organizing consultant. They're often stuck with the "clean up before the maid comes" syndrome, or they are concerned about how to prepare for his or her arrival.

Put aside any worries about needing to justify your situation. The organizing consultant's role is to provide professional advice, not to make judgments. Ask yourself the questions: "Why did I make this appointment with an organizing consultant?" and "What do I want to change?"

It is not *necessary* to do anything, but *if* you feel a need to get started before the consultant comes, here are some suggestions.

- The consultant will begin work immediately, so choose where you would like to begin—with today's mail or the attic.
- Gather together any supplies you may have on hand that will be helpful in the organizing process—file folder, labels, marking pens, boxes, containers, wastebaskets, etc.
- Put all like things together—banking information, photographs, magazines, etc.

Relax! If you're unsure about where to begin or what to do, your organizing consultant has the knowledge and experience to guide you in making that decision.

## What Can You Expect from an Organizing Consultant?

The first step in developing a good working relationship with an organizing consultant is to have a realistic understanding of what you can and should expect.
- Complete confidentiality.
- Open discussion about the cost of services.
- Appointments scheduled to meet your professional and/or personal needs.
- An ability to apply the "principles of organization" to your particular situation.
- Expertise and experience in the "principles of organization" applied to personal and professional life.
- Creative and innovative problem solving.
- A willingness to do whatever task needs to be done in the interest of achieving mutually determined goals.
- Physical assistance, as well as verbal instruction. A willingness to do whatever you would do—including getting dirty!
- Shopping assistance if you need or want it.
- Assistance in finding another professional resource if it is appropriate or desirable.
- Availability and a continued interest in your situation, should you desire.

*It is always easier to see what someone else needs to do than it is to see what we need to do.*

There are hundreds of organizing consultants in the country, and more are being trained everyday. The exciting aspect of the industry is the networking that takes place among the organizers themselves. Not all organizers provide the same services so keep looking until you find the one that suits your needs and your personality. If the first one you try doesn't work, don't give up!

## A Note of Caution

It is always easier to see what someone else needs to do than it is to see what we need to do. In teaching organizing skills to families, one of my key roles is to insure that family members concentrate on solving their own organizing problems instead of what other family members need to do. As you read this book and experiment with developing new paper-management systems for yourself, resist the urge to insist that other people join you. Many of the systems you develop will automatically make paper management easier for other people, but let them discover it for themselves!

If you are interested in sponsoring a seminar on organizing in your area, or you know someone who might be, feel free to write or call me at Hemphill & Associates, Inc. 2020 Pennsylvania Ave., NW, Suite 171, Washington, D.C. 20006, 202-387-8007.

Although you are at the end of this book, you are at the beginning of a new adventure in learning to control the paper in your life. Remember, "In every organizing process, things will get worse before they get better." Try to remain optimistic. Forgive yourself when you see the mistakes you have made in the past and move on. Feeling bad about yourself does not help anything. Be willing to ask for help when you need it, and reward yourself for each accomplishment along the way. Now grab that tiger by the tail! You are on your way to a personal paper-management system that works for you!

# Appendix:
# Records Locator
# and Retention Guide

Thoughout this book I've written about different kinds of paper that you need to keep—or might want to keep. The locator and retention guide on the following pages will serve as a quick reference tool for you to use to identify your papers and note where you keep them and how long they need to be retained. Check the index for references to detailed discussions about ways to deal with the various documents. Then fill out the worksheet, and keep it in a handy location. Also make a copies for people in your life who might need the information in case of emergency.

In many cases, it's up to you where you want to keep a document and how long you decide to hold on to it. I've indicated a specific location and/or retention guideline when there is a legal requirement—or I've felt it would be helpful to do so.

Keep in mind that where you keep documents is not nearly as important as doing it consistently. Problems develop when part of the information you need is in one location and part is in another. However, because of space considerations it may sometimes be necessary to put documents in more than one place. When this happens, be sure to note both locations on this guide. For example, old tax records could be stored in the attic while the most recent year's records could be in your reference file.

Be sure to include a timetable for transferring records from active to inactive storage or disposal. (A good time to do this would be after you file your income tax return.) You may find that the least complicated method for keeping records is to put all records for a given year into a large envelope or box and store them in chronological order. When you put in the latest year's records, take out unneeded or unwanted material from earlier years.

| Document | Location | Retain how long |
|---|---|---|
| **Education Records** | | |
| Certificates | _____ | _____ |
| Diplomas | _____ | _____ |
| Letters of reference | _____ | Update periodically |
| Resumes | _____ | Until superceded |
| _____ | _____ | _____ |
| _____ | _____ | _____ |
| | | |
| **Health Records** | | |
| Illness records | _____ | Permanently |
| Vaccination records | _____ | Permanently |
| _____ | _____ | _____ |
| _____ | _____ | _____ |
| | | |
| **Insurance** | | |
| Automobile | _____ | Statute of limitations, in case of late claims |
| Disability | _____ | Duration of policy |
| Health | _____ | Duration of policy |
| Homeowner's | _____ | Statute of limitations, in case of late claims |
| Liability | _____ | Statute of limitations, in case of late claims |
| Life | Safe deposit box | Duration of policy |
| Personal property | _____ | Duration of policy |
| Umbrella policy | _____ | Duration of policy |
| _____ | _____ | _____ |
| _____ | _____ | _____ |
| | | |
| **Investments** | | |
| Purchase records | _____ | As long as you own security, then keep with sale record |
| Sales records | _____ | Six years after sale, for tax purposes |
| Home improvements | _____ | Until you purchase again, then with tax records |

| Document | Location | Retain how long |
|---|---|---|
| Collectibles | _____ | As long as you own, then with tax records |
| Household inventory | _____ | Update annually |
| Mortgage information | _____ | 6 years after sale |
| _____ | _____ | _____ |
| _____ | _____ | _____ |

**Military records**

| | | |
|---|---|---|
| Discharge papers | Safe deposit box | Permanently |

**Personal property records**

| | | |
|---|---|---|
| Automobile registration | Copy in car; original with driver | As long as you own auto |
| Receipts for major purchases | _____ | As long as you own item |
| _____ | _____ | _____ |
| _____ | _____ | _____ |

**Personal life**

| | | |
|---|---|---|
| Calendars (past) | _____ | _____ |
| Directories | _____ | _____ |
| Letters/greeting cards received | _____ | _____ |
| Memorabilia | _____ | _____ |
| Photographs | _____ | _____ |
| Religious records | _____ | _____ |
| _____ | _____ | _____ |
| _____ | _____ | _____ |
| _____ | _____ | _____ |

**Pet records**

| | | |
|---|---|---|
| _____ | _____ | _____ |

**Tax & financial**

| | | |
|---|---|---|
| Bank statements | _____ | 6 years |
| Canceled checks | _____ | 6 years, if for deductible item |

# APPENDIX

| Document | Location | Retain how long |
|----------|----------|-----------------|
| Certificates of deposit | _____ | Until cashed in |
| Contracts | _____ | 6 years after completion |
| Credit card statements/receipts | _____ | 6 years, if for deductible item |
| Income tax returns | _____ | Generally 6 years. Exceptions: non-deductible IRA form and records of home improvements (indefinitely) |
| Income tax support documents | _____ | Same as above |
| Loan agreements | _____ | 6 years after payment |
| Loan payment books | _____ | Until paid |
| Pension plan records | _____ | Generally keep current year only |
| Rental contracts | _____ | As long as in effect |
| Pay stub | _____ | Until W-2 confirmed |
| Trust agreements | _____ | As long as in effect |

**Vital records**

| | | |
|----------|----------|-----------------|
| Adoption papers | Safe deposit box | Permanently |
| Automobile title | Safe deposit box | As long as you own car |
| Birth certificates | Safe deposit box | Permanently |
| Citizenship papers | Safe deposit box | Permanently |
| Copyrights/patents | Safe deposit box | As long as in effect |
| Death certificates | Safe deposit box | Until estate is settled |
| Divorce decrees | Safe deposit box | Permanently |
| Letter of last instructions | _____ | Permanently. Update as needed. |
| Marriage certificate | Safe deposit box | Permanently |
| Passports | _____ | Keep current |
| Power of attorney | _____ | Permanently. Update as needed |
| Safe deposit box key | _____ | As long as you keep box |
| Safe deposit box inventory | _____ | Update regularly |

APPENDIX

| Document | Location | Retain how long |
|---|---|---|
| Social security records | _____ | Permanently |
| Wills | _____ | As long as valid |
| _____ | _____ | _____ |
| _____ | _____ | _____ |
| _____ | _____ | _____ |

**Warranties & instructions**

| | | |
|---|---|---|
| _____ | _____ | As long as you own appliance or device |
| _____ | _____ | _____ |

# Index

## A

Action files
  bill paying and, 63, 96
  categories, 60–66
  checklist, 61
  description, 58, 59
  logistics of, 66–67
  "To Do" list and, 67
  for travel, 65, 169
Aging family members. *See*
    Ill or aging family
    members
Airline files, 166
Answering machines,
    146–147
Appliance instructions,
    130–131
Automobile insurance, 125

## B

Bank records, 122
Bills
  action files and, 63, 96
  credit card receipts, 97–98
  electronic payment, 95
  payment schedule, 95–96
  statements, 97
  tracking, 94–95
  work area for paying,
    96–97
Birthdays
  "To Do" list, 49
  "To Write" file, 119–120
Bonds, 123
Bulletin boards
  phone messages, 145
  specific purpose, 22

Burial instructions, 128
Business car logbook, 105
Businesses
  correspondence, 120
  records to keep, 123

## C

Calendars
  birthdays, 119
  children and, 161–162
  computer software for,
    173
  day-on-a-page sample,
    43
  electronic, 41
  entering information,
    38–39
  events calendar, 65
  making appointments
    with yourself, 39–40,
    110
  master calendar, 37–38
  month-on-a-page sample,
    42
  reward for return, 41
  schedule coordination
    and, 38
  selection factors, 40–41
  symbols, 39, 67
  telephone numbers, 55
Cards. *See* Credit cards;
    Greeting cards;
    Holiday card lists
Car-rental bonus programs,
    167
Catalog shopping, 111
Chairs, 20–21
Charge accounts. *See*
    Credit cards

Children's papers
  assignment books, 162
  calendars, 161–162
  categories, 158–159
  child's own files, 91, 163
  creative papers, 160–161
  index for, 163
  involving children in
    decision making,
    159–160
  memorabilia box, 161
Collectibles, 123
Computers
  action files and, 62
  bill paying software,
    95–96
  file index, 172–173
  hard copy vs. computer
    copy, 173–174
  kitchen uses, 151
  location, 21
  notebook computers,
    41
  organizing files, 174–175
  records tracking, 173
  software options, 173
  storing printed reports,
    172
  supplies, 23
  telephone number
    program, 54
  "To Do" list software,
    47
Condolence letters, 118–119
Coupons, 155–156
Credit cards
  receipts, 97–98
  records needed, 122
  reducing number of, 96

# INDEX